THE MAKING OF A MARTIAL ARTIST

THE MAKING OF A MARTIAL ARTIST

BY: SANG KYU SHIM

Photography by Leo Knight

Design by Skyline Studios, Inc.
16265 Meyers Rd., Detroit, MI 48235

First Edition
U.S. Library of Congress Cataloging in Publication Data.

Also by Sang Kyu Shim

Promise and Fulfillment in the Art of Tae Kwon Do.
Published in 1974

For information, address:

Sang Kyu Shim
17625 W. 7 Mile Rd.
Detroit, Michigan 48235

CONTENTS

Sang Kyu Shim

AUTHOR'S FOREWORD

The purpose of this book is to focus on the true nature of the martial arts: what they are, their source, how they developed, their underlying philosophy, and their future prospects.

Much more than sport, display, or means to money, they are concerned with more than physical fitness, fighting skills, and conditioning. While the martial arts do, indeed, involve physique, they are more concerned with the why, how, where, and when of physical involvement. They predicate a philosophic foundation through which they ultimately become a way of life. They decompartmentalize living so that the same principle energizes every moment. While following their pattern, one sets oneself free.

The place of the individual can be seen from two basic viewpoints. On the one hand, he is a unique being, freely making choices and willing his own destiny; on the other, he is a mere atom, completely dominated by the gigantic flow of universal forces. Which view a person adopts will profoundly influence all the rest of his life. The differences between success and failure lies in one's self-concept.

The martial arts project the more positive self-image, allowing the practitioner to assume responsibility for what he is, and to claim the just rewards of creative action. In their fullness, the martial arts defend the independent spirit as much as the well-being of the body. The master of the martial arts is, essentially, not a "sayer," but a "doer."

The process of re-assessment is built into the very nature and goals of the martial arts. An understanding of and appreciation for their history and tradition are essential to their proper practice and mission. It is my sincere hope that this book will open to many the road to creative change, the road to encounter and discovery, the road to fulfillment and happiness. The journey begins with a single step; the way itself is endless. Much of its achievement is in the process, for, as someone once said, perfection closes the door.

To all my readers I wish the challenge, reward, joy, and pleasure of setting out and reaching the goal on the way of the martial arts.

Chapter 1

INTRODUCTION

*What a piece of work is man! how noble in reason! how
infinite in faculties! in form and moving how express and
admirable! in action how like an angel! in apprehension
how like a god! the beauty of the world, the paragon of
animals!*

Shakespeare, Hamlet

In an age of computerization and inter-planetary powers, it is more imperative than ever for man to re-think his identity and his values. Socrates' age-old dictum: Know thyself! is still a challenge. Man must know his splendor, he must know his weakness.

His splendor? in the whole universe, it is the creature *man* who embodies the cosmos. He has within himself the elements of every order: the inanimate, the organic, the rational, and the spiritual. Each on a different plane, none is important. The lower planes form a beginning for the higher planes to function. Yet, no faculty functions in isolation: all act in totality. Who has ever been able to separate heat and light in a flame? Still, heat and light are distinct entities. So the being, man. His splendor is the unity and interaction of all his faculties.

His weakness? what is man against the grandeur of space, the hugeness of a mountain, or the vastness of the sea? What is he beside the power of lightning, of the wind, and the waves? How dependent he is on the sun's energy, and how helpless at the onslaught of a single virus or a freak accident! By chemical composition, man is worth approximately ninety-eight cents (give or take the differences inflation makes).

More humiliating is man's potential for moral and spiritual degradation. The world is full of misery caused by man's choice to be selfish, unjust, prejudiced, short-sighted. His boast of freedom—free will—is conditioned on every side by environment, genetics, politics, and economics. What chance do the poor have among the rich, the handicapped among the healthy, the moronic among geniuses?

Yet these potentials to failure are the very means man has to success. So he is conditioned: this applies only to the "accidental" features of life. The will to overcome weakness, the effort to gain control and to the achievement of final victory over self and his environment is man's ultimate glory.

Naturally, such fulfillment is a never-ending process. Development demands time and constant effort. Shakespeare speaks of the seven stages in the life of any human: from "the infant, mewling and puking in his nurse's arms" to "second childishness...sans teeth, sans eyes, sans taste, sans everything." *(As You Like It.)* Not a very flattering picture, especially in that there is no mention of the virtues of humanity: love, honor, loyalty. Yet the development of virtuous action makes all the difference. A proper balance of the two extremes, human transience and expendability, provide permanence and lasting perpetuation in mankind.

The limitations imposed by chronological time are more than offset by the use of psychological time. The latter is the only kind of much worth. Many an 80-year-old person has never matured, and many a teenager has the wisdom of an octagenarian. Not the event, but how one uses the event, is important.

For this, introspection is the key, for it shows mind, not matter; active choice, not passive existence; growth, not decay; life, not death. Sight is good, but it is meaningless without perception.

What has all this to do with the martial arts? Everything! Life is change. To have changed often is to have lived much. The martial arts use given social structures to fit the individual's needs. Through continuous examination of values, through persistent and consistent effort, through an informed and imaginative re-setting of sights, the martial arts form and reform its faithful practitioners. Re-forming the individual re-forms society. The riddle of life is never solved definitively; its solution lies outside space and time. Vital issues always remain open. This is the challenge of life. This is the challenge the martial artist enthuiastically takes up and vanquishes.

Chapter **2**

WHAT ARE THE MARTIAL ARTS?

*To everything there is a season and a time for every affair
under the heavens. A time to be born, and a time to die; a
time to plant, and a time to uproot the plant. A time to kill,
and a time to heal; a time to tear down, and a time to build.
A time to weep, and a time to laugh; a time to mourn, and
a time to dance. A time to scatter stones, and a time to
gather them; a time to embrace, and a time to be far from
embrace. A time to seek, and a time to lose; a time to keep,
and a time to cast away. A time to rend, and a time to sew;
a time to be silent, and a time to speak. A time to love, and
a time to hate; a time of war, and a time of peace.*
Ecclesiates:

Oriental martial arts have recently seen a rapid upsurge in Western civilization. They have now become popular in every corner of the world. Are they simply a point of curiosity to Westerners, a fad to be discarded once the novelty has worn off? Is their popularity to be ascribed to the need for self-defense in a world of increasing violence? Is there a current vogue for following non-Western cults?[1]

The answers to these questions require more than a cursory look or a quick definition. The questions involve the *whole* person in the *whole* world: the nature of each and the mutual demands of both, here and now. The martial arts reflect a human and cultural enterprise to be explored. The boundaries between these two pursuits are notoriously vague; hence, a clarification of certain basic ideas is necessary before a direct treatment of the answers is possible.

Let's say, a gardener is offered a plot of fertile soil and an abundance of seeds. He is to raise vegetables. Before he can plant, he must root out weeds and rid the plot of foreign matter.

Analogously, the answer to "What are the martial arts?" cannot begin until popular misconceptions are cleared away. That is, what are the martial arts *not*?

First, they are not a security blanket. In today's world of multi-corporations and tight governmental structures—a world where might too often prevails over right—the individual seems to count for less and less. This condition breeds not only a sense of insecurity in the individual, but a loss of identity; one counts only insofar as one is related to an organized group: the Club, the Gang, the Association, the Cult, whatever the "in thing" happens to be. Even when one wishes to preserve a sense of self, the tendency to stereotype is all too prevalent. How often one hears expressions like "that teenaged punk," "that over-thirty has-been," "the pig," "the stupid farmer." Self is threatened at every turn, and consequently, individuals adopt fighting skills as a means to assert themselves. The martial arts provide a means of self-defense or even, should this be necessary, of aggressive behavior. But if this is all they provide, then the user has sold himself short of the better part of the martial arts.

Secondly, the martial arts do not mean conformity. While training demands a certain amount of imitation of form and basic routines, these are only the beginning. A strong house must have a firm foundation, but the foundation is not the house. The object of training is not to turn out robots or assembly-line products. The martial arts point, first, last and always, to the uniqueness of the individual. An operative base is established by imitation of a master form. However, once this is achieved (and in the course of its achieving),the student is encouraged, even commanded, to build on his own, to adapt the means to his needs, his personality, his place in society.

Thirdly, the martial arts are not mere sport, despite a superficial resemblance between the two. Some enthusiasts would like to see the martial arts included in Olympic competitions. This is contrary to the nature and spirit of the martial arts. Commendable as the Olympics may be as a form of international competition, they are not a way of life, as the martial arts, in their true sense, are. Sport may be a career, but it is limited to a given span of time, and to a given form of activity. The person excels in a particular skill, say in hockey; as long as he is better than others in this skill, so long and no longer will he be professionally active. The martial arts, by contrast, extend into every act one performs throughout one's lifetime.

The martial arts, further, are certainly not intended as some form of idle entertainment. The feats of David Caradine in the popular Kung-fu series may be spectacular, but the martial arts are not a spectacle. Through a mistaken sense of identification with a "hero," hordes of Kung-fu fans took up classes in various forms of unarmed combat, only to give them up when the real work began.[2] The study of martial arts cannot be put on and taken off like a garment; they cannot be a role-playing performance. They cannot be adopted and rejected as one steps into or out of a theatrical part.

The martial arts are most particularly not a political device. Their practice spans the world, knowing no boundaries. When they are looked on as serving political victory, or when used to humiliate political opponents, their users are in direct contradiction to the prime purpose of the martial arts. Recent events in Olympic history, for instance, show how supposedly total a-political activities have been made tools to serve base political ends.[3]

Finally, the martial arts are not a skill leading to street-fighting and other forms of illegal violence. To use the arts for vice fundamentally opposes their aim. If, in fact, a student of the martial arts takes up training with the intention of becoming a street-fighter, he must soon give up the notion of street-fighting or give up his study, because no martial arts master will keep a student who would bring his art into such disrepute. On the other hand, skill in unarmed combat can save lives, should one unfortunately, be caught in violence requiring defensive fighting. One need not reject the benefits of an art because they are its by-products rather than its main objective.

The martial arts are closely related to philosophy, religion, science, and arts, insofar as they attempt to establish human life in some satisfying and meaningful relation to the universe, and to afford some wisdom in the conduct of human affairs.

The martial arts are "religious" in that an inherent element in them is the development of moral character. A negatively motivated mind with intent merely to destroy is immoral. A positively motivated mind makes the seemingly impossible possible. In their capacity as art, as a physical exercise, and as a spiritual discipline, the martial arts are a method of unifying matter and spirit in such a way as infinitely to broaden and deepen human life.

In the matter of method, the martial arts are allied to science. They are demonstrable, capable of analysis, and functional. They are revitalized by fresh contact, concepts, methods, and standards. They are scientific in their use of anatomical data as well as in their organic development. They are intelligible, logical, and highly structured in both form and content. Their techniques are precisely definable in space and time.

Artistically designed, the martial arts hold a firm place among all art. The outstanding martial artists are those endowed with something akin to poetic imagination, critical acumen, natural piety, and spiritual insight. Martial art is a form of applied art, aesthetically as demanding as ballet and as time-demanding as sculpting.

On the other hand, the martial arts are not just another form of philosophy, religion, science, or art. They differ from philosophy in that they are more than theory; from religion in that they make no claim to being supernatural; from science in that they accept certain realities as inexplicable in purely scientific terms; and finally, from art in that they are not intransient as music or color.

The martial arts begin with the acceptance of self, "I" as I am, unique, one of a kind.

> One great splitting of the whole universe into two halves is made
> by each of us, and for each of us almost all the interest to one
> of the halves; but we all draw the line of division between them
> in a different place. When I say that we all call the two halves
> by the same names, and that those names are "me" and "not
> me" respectively, it will at once be seen what I mean.[4]

The martial arts attempt to define this paradoxical self, to defend it against all encroachment, and then give it up at the point where it is finally gained. While things about one change, the "I" remains constant until the "I" itself succumbs to change and extinction in death. Still, when one considers the "not me" one moves from outer space, stars, to mountains, to persons one knows, to one's own limbs, to one's specific "me-ness," and one finally arrives at "nothing." Thus the paradox: the distinction between the "me" and the "not me" is at once identical and illusory. The martial arts, accepting the paradox, say equally paradoxically: either one has no self to defend, or one has nothing to defend the self from. So (one may ask), why look to defend "nothing"?

The martial arts espouse more than abstractions or theories. Before one can realize the "nothing" or the "I," one must embark on a most intense search for the true self, through physical discipline and mental cultivation. While man is mortal, he aspires to immortality. Is this immortality some-thing or no-thing? Is it a new life order or is it oblivion? The martial arts, when fully practised, point to this eternal theme, not hesitating to contend with paradox if it must. Hence, one must take a closer look at how "immortality" is understood.

Three general modes of immortality have been expressed: the biological, the theological, and the psychical (for lack of a better word).

The biological is the most immediate and the most obvious. It is the sense of living on through and in one's posterity. At some level of consciousness one can imagine an endless chain of contingent attachments. This mode has been a classical expression of symbolic immortality in East Asian culture, especially in traditional China and its emphasis on ancestor worship. The individual man dies, but mankind goes on. In Confucian ethics the greatest of all unfilial acts is the failure to produce offspring. This biological mode is limited to the purely biological. What happens, for instance, if by infertility or accident, the family line is broken? In a way, this difficulty is overcome if one allows the mode to extend to the bio-social, expressing itself in attachments to one's group, tribe, organization, people, nation or even species. Anyone can ultimately feel at least glimmerings of immortality through his species. Martial art, originating in the Orient, cannot be separated from Confucian ethics. Insofar as children become identified as parents themselves (the family being the basic social unit), one's socio-biological self is extended infinitely—that is, one achieves "immortality."

The theological mode looks to life after death; that is, the individual is released from a tangible existence, to a life on a higher plane. Since, by definition, no one can explain what this higher plane consists of, a literal notion of it is impossible. More important and fundamental to it is the concept of spiritual transcendence over death, as exemplified in the great religions founded by Buddha, Christ, Moses, and Mohammed. The Japanese word *Kami*, the Polynesian term *mana*, the Roman idea *noumen*, the Eskimo concept *tungnik*, and the Christian doctrine of *grace*—all describe a state wherein one possesses spiritual power over death. Symbolically (to some people, actually), this transcendence reflects one's harmony with a principle extending beyond the limited biological life-span. In martial art this sense of immortality is accepted not by claiming that its practice can "earn" an afterlife, but by understanding the concept of transcendence over death through spiritual attachment, one can supersede the material self in favor of the spiritual which never dies. Therefore, the "immortality" fostered by the martial arts consists in the cultivation of inner solitude, by meditation and concentration. Soul-communing can and does extend the mortal (tangible) to the immortal (intangible to sense).

The third expression of immortality—the psychical—differs from the other two in that it depends almost exclusively on a psychic state. This state is "experiential transcendence," a state so intense that in it, time and death apparently disappear. Characterized by extraordinary psychic unity and perceptual acuity, this state has been poetically and religiously described as "losing one-self." It occurs not only in religious mysticism, but also in song, dance, battle, sexual love, childbirth, athletic effort, and mechanical flight. It can also occur in the contemplation of beauty and in intellectual creation. Its reality is proven in that, returning from this state, the individual feels "different;" something in his "self" has been changed. Experiential transcendence includes a feeling of what Mercia Eliade has called the "continuous present," which can be equated with eternity or with "mythical time."[5] This continuous present is perceived not only as the "here and now," but as inseparable from the past and future. It is through meditation (most deeply brought about by a system of abdominal breathing featured in the practice of the martial arts[6]) that one can enjoy mythical time and mythical space, extending one's existence beyond the tangible world.

Of the three expressions of immortality just described, the martial arts focus mainly on the third: transcendence. Most people are not living as much as they can. Physiologically and spiritually, human potential far exceeds its actual use. The martial artist strives to find the secret of being able to live fully in the continuous present, not momentarily, but always. There is no advantage in a long life (measured chronologically) if it is an unfulfilled life. The martial arts seek to bring to flower man's capacity for fulfillment—that is, his capacity for happiness.

The sense of life is clear to a happy person. Such a person lives in the present and has no fear, not even in the face of death. A happy person can renounce the amenities of the world.[7]

A man who is happy in his marriage and his children is not likely to feel much envy of other men because of their greater wealth or success, so long as he has enough to bring up his children in what he feels to be the right way. The essentials of human happiness are simple, so simple that sophisticated people cannot bring themselves to admit what it is they really lack.[8]

The martial arts are not an irrational pursuit; yet they are not obsessively concerned with rational justification and proofs for the existence of soul or spirit. While human understanding is limited, immortality, by definition, is not limited by reason. Even though man aspires to be immortal, no one can adequately account for this desire. "Disembodied person" is a vacuous concept because mind and body together make one whole.

The happy man has no fear of death and has no need of proof of immortality. The Bible puts it succinctly: What does it profit a man to gain the whole world and suffer the loss of his soul?[9]

For the martial artist, happiness is not something to be had only in the afterlife. It is not only desirable, but very possible, to begin it and maintain it *now*. The person who lives in the continuous present need not "go" anywhere; he simply resides actively in his part of nature. Having lived in a natural way, he dies in a natural way, for in nature nothing is lost or wasted.[10]

Favor, like disgrace
Brings trouble with it;
High rank, like self,
Involves acute distress.

What does that mean, to say
That"favor, like disgrace
Brings trouble with it"?
When favor is bestowed
On one of low degree,

Trouble will come with it.
The loss of favor too
Means trouble for that man.
This, then, is meant
By "favor, like disgrace
Brings trouble with it."

What does it mean, to say
That "rank, like self,
Involves acute distress"?
I suffer most because
Of me and selfishness.
If I were selfless, then
What suffering would I bear?

In governing the world,
Let rule entrusted be
To him who treats his rank
As if it were his soul;
World sovereignty can be
Committed to that man
Who loves all people
As he loves himself.
—Lao-Tze

Many individuals are hounded by a sense of alienation. The individual

tries to solve the problem...by conforming. He feels secure in
being as similar as possible to his fellow man. His paramount
aim is to be approved of by others; his central fear, that he
may not be approved of. To be different, to find himself in a
minority, are the dangers which threaten his sense of security;
hence a craving for limitless conformity. [11]

The martial arts urge: Be unique! Dare not to conform! They are the means to self-confidence, achieved through three essential powers: inner power or uniqueness, outer power or technique, and spiritual power or moral perfection. These allow the individual mastery.

Does this mean living in an idealistic world, having nothing to do with the realistic? No, not at all! Having ideals is not incompatible with realism. An interesting anecdote relating to Thales, the philosopher, illustrates the point. The warehouses of Thales' home town, Miletus, were stocked with goods from all over the world. Money having become the universal means of exchange, it was a highly regarded possession. On one occasion Thales' practicality was challenged: could a "thinker" also be a "money-maker"? As it happened, Thales' grasp of meteorology enabled him to foresee that the olive harvest would be rich. He rented all available oil-presses long before they were needed; at harvest time, he sub-let them at his own price. The ensuing fortune silenced his scoffers, showing them that idealists need not be impractical.

On the other hand, practical persons need not be without their ideals. The point may again be illustrated by an example. One morning in 1888 Alfred Nobel, who had by then amassed a fortune from the manufacture and sale of firearms, awoke to read his own obituary. The notice was, of course, a journalistic error; it was Alfred's brother who had died. Still, the shock was overwhelming to Alfred. He suddenly realized how the world would remember him: the "dynamite king," the industrialist who became rich by selling explosives! "What of my other works?" he thought. "What of my humanitarian acts, my attempts to dissolve the barriers between men and ideas, between nation and nation? Are these to be forgotten? Am I to be best remembered as a merchant of death?" He resolved to change his memorial. His last will and testament would be the expression of his life's ideals. Thus was established the Nobel Peace Prize, the one given those who have done most for the advancement of world peace and of making a better world.

The martial arts espouse a balanced blend of the ideal and the real world. Ideas and actions are tools. The martial arts are a tool both for defending self and for realizing self. Unfortunately, it is possible to stop before reaching the goal; the blame for the resulting loss should in that case not be attributed to the tool, but to the misuse of the tool.

The permeation of one's every act, no matter how mundane or exalted, is the proper function of the martial arts. This virtue of permeation might be compared to the use of an overall natural health aid, such as ginseng. This is a powerful and, some say, mystical oriental drug; mystical, because no one knows *how* it cures; powerful, because no presently known drug is more effective in therapeutic value, with no harmful side-effects. Sweet, and slightly cool to the taste, ginseng (according to traditional oriental medical texts) is a tonic to the five viscera. It quiets the spirit, stabilizes the soul, allays fears, expels evil effluvia, brightens the eyes, improves understanding, and, if taken over an extended period of time, invigorates the body and prolongs life. Even more recent tests show undeniably that the use of ginseng helps maintain a clear mental state, stabilizes the mind, and promotes good digestion. Furthermore, it has a marked effect in the treatment of ailments of the mucous membranes of the stomach.[12] However, it is not used to heal broken arms or to extract shrapnel. It is useful only in the promotion of general mental and physical health.

So it is with the martial arts. Like ginseng, the martial arts cannot successfully be used to achieve one's particular self-interests. They will not put hair on one's chest or change a homely person into a ravishing beauty. Rather, they promote a general well-being in all one does and thinks. They are a way of life. The mysterious development resulting from following this way is as inexplicable as are the long-and-short term effects of ginseng.[13]

One must not confuse the skills of living with the way of living. The martial arts point the way while providing the skills needed to follow the way. This is the road to creative change, a road of encounter and discovery; it is the road of a million miles that begins with the first step.[14] If each individual advances to self-actualization, willingly sharing his finds, one can be optimistic about the improvement of life. Instead of fragmenting and destroying human potential, one invests it for the continuing present. In this way, one controls the direction in which life (and the world) will go.

The martial artist learns to appreciate the doing itself; the process never ends. Every time he reaches a goal, a new one appears. He keeps open the doors of creativity, awareness, and spontaneity. Security for him rests not in splendid isolation but in mutual interaction with others. His inner solitude is something he chooses out of a desire for privacy, an occasion for deep reflection, not an enforced or stultifying confinement.

Does the proper application of martial art mean a negation of wealth, entertainment, self-defense, or physical fitness? No! Martial art may well include these features, but they are not its prime end. They are by-products of its essential elements. One may, indeed, amass a fortune while practising the martial arts; indeed, a currency-conscious world demands that one have some money sense. It can be a means to sharing the ideals of the martial arts. One frees oneself from the pervading sense of alienation in the world, and gains a true sense of self-identity and self-worth.

The martial arts can be a potent means of self-defense. They are a far cry, however, from the fads of the day, for the martial artist is searching not for mere resistance to injury, but for self-realization, whatever that may entail. He is searching for perfection, conscious of his strengths and weaknesses. This knowledge is a first step that will keep him constantly striving to augment the strengths and diminish the weaknesses.[15]

It is almost impossible for a man of character not to be publicly recognized. Hence, it is quite possible that he be almost forced into public service. Again, there is nothing contradictory between the martial arts and political involvement. The caution is to keep them in the proper perspective. [16] The martial artist is the total man who

> does not expose himself needlessly to danger since there are few things for which he cares sufficiently (to do that); but he is willing in great crises to give even his life—knowing that under certain conditions it is not worthwhile to live. He is of a disposition to do men service, though he is ashamed to require service of others. To confer a kindness is a mark of superiority....(The superior man) does not take part in public displays. [17]

A person in the public eye has all the more reason to be of sound character. Being talented in sports, politics, or as an entertainer does not condone moral decreptitude. Those who identify the martial arts only with power over others must go back and learn from the beginning.

As the good of the sportsman is success in sport, that of the philosopher logical thought, and that of the businessman to make profit, so is it the good of the martial artist to realize his fullest potential physically, mentally, and spiritually. The harmonious organization of his faculties represents a development for all of society, for man's fulfillment is essentially rooted in his being individually and collectively moral. If the martial arts do not effect this, they are nothing.

In sum, then, what are the martial arts?

The martial arts are a way of life. They are a means to creative self-actualization and service to others. In their proper exercise they provide the necessary discipline, control, and fortitude needed in the pursuit of perfection and the realization of virtue in everyday life.

It is a truism that any characteristic of a person cannot be segregated from the conglomerate formed by all the characteristics of that person. Therefore, any trait, whether a vice or a virtue, will affect the whole person. So the martial arts, even in their physical aspects, are continuously aimed at total development; in their ultimate objective, and as an integral part of daily living, they bring spiritual fulfillment and peace.

NOTES TO CHAPTER 2

1. Susan Leslie. "Coming on Strong," *Weekend Magazine,* August 11, 1979 (Editorial offices: Suite 504, 390 Bay Street, Toronto), pp. 14-16. While the whole article applies, a small excerpt from the experience of a martial artist, Dulce Oikawa, is enlightening. She is 37, the mother of a 10-year-old boy, and an employee of the British Columbia Teachers' Federation. Dulce's introduction to the martial art of karate came through a self-defense class. She is 5'2" and weighs 110 pounds, but in a karate class she looks formidable. "As soon as I go into karate class, everything becomes focused. Karate has really helped me to see that there's a mind and a body and a spirit, and to be a true karate person (i.e., a martial artist), there has to be a harmony of the three. I've gone beyond that need for self-defence, and as I've worked with karate the appeal has become very aesthetic. It's a real art, and it's a way of looking at life."

2. At one point in his career, Glen Gould insisted on bringing his own piano-stool wherever he performed. Hence, piano students all over the country refused to come to lessons without their own piano stools tucked under their arms. This was going to help them play like Glenn Gould? Mr. Gould was a great artist in spite of his eccentricity, not because of it.

3. During the 1972 Olympics in Munich, Arab terrorists broke into the residence of Israeli athletes and brutally murdered them.

4. Henry James. *Principles of Psychology,* I, p. 289.

5. Mercia Eliade. *Myths, Dreams, and Mysteries* (Harper and Row, New York and Evanston, 1957) pp. 106 ff. Transcendance is related to the idea of flight in order to achieve freedom..."the roots of freedom are to be sought in the depths of the psyche...the desire for absolute freedom ranks among the essential longings of man, irrespective of the stage his culture has reached and of its form of social organization. The creation, repeated to infinity, of these countless imaginary universes in which space is transcended and weight is abolished, speaks volumes upon the true nature of the human being. The longing to break the ties that hold him in bondage to earth is not a result of cosmic pressures or of economic insecurity—it is constitutive of man, in that he is a being who enjoys a mode of existence unique in the world....(There is) a longing to see the human body behaving like a "spirit," to transmute the corporeal modality of man into a spiritual modality...whatever be the content and the value ascribed to ascensional experience...there remain always the two essential motifs—transcendance and freedom, both the one and the other obtained by a rupture of the plane of experience, and experience of an ontological mutation of the human being. It is because they no longer partake of the human condition, and in so far as they are "free" that the Sovereigns are supposed to be able to fly through the air. It is for the same reason that the yogis, the alchemists, the *arhat,* are able to transport themselves at will, to fly, or to disappear."

6. Abdominal breathing is given a longer treatment in Chapter 11.

7. Wittengenstein. *Notebooks 1914-16,* pp. 73-74.

8. Bertrand Russell. *Autobiography,* p. 78.

9. History is filled with examples of persons who "had everything going for them," yet ended their lives in suicide. Current examples are Marilyn Monroe and Freddie Prinz.

10. One place in the world where one finds happy people is the small nation of Hunza, located in West Pakistan, sixty-five miles northeast of Gilgit, eighteen miles south of the Soviet Union, in the heart of the Himalayas. Surrounded by impassable mountain ranges, it is accessible only by foot. Only 100 miles long by two miles wide, with a population of 25,000, Hunza has gone unchanged in geography books until just recently.

The people of Hunza still exist isolated from the world where they live to be 120 to 140 years old with literally no cancer, heart attacks, or other major disorders. Active and fit

NOTES TO CHAPTER 2

to the very end, men father children at 100 years and older; overweight people are unheard of. Hunza elders also have perfect health, teeth, eyesight, mental abilities, full heads of hair, and can walk a 65-mile mountain trail with full pack, and immediately start working in the fields again. Hunza women likewise have perfect health, figures, and complexions. Hunza women of eighty look like American women of forty, their complexion secret lying in an oil from a certain fruit with which they are able to avoid getting wrinkles. A natural skin preserver, the oil is said to remove a deposit which is responsible for wrinkles.

Hunza sounds like a Utopia, having no disease, no psychological disorders, no divorce, no juvenile delinquency, no greed, and no jealousy. There has not been a crime reported in 130 years. These people do not know what one means by cancer, heart disease, arthritis, neurosis, rapes, muggings, or murder. How do they die? Everything goes very quickly and all at once—no sickness and suffering. That is the natural way. The stories of Hunza defy belief. But those who visited Hunza in the '50's and '60's would not be the type to lie. Each visitor, including such notables as Chou En Lai and Queen Elizabeth, came back with the same findings.

A modern witness is C.W. Nicol. In *Moving Zen* (William Morrow and Co., 1975), p. 144, he writes: Shimizu sensei was now in his seventies, yet with a sweep of his white oak stick he could either knock the sword out of my hand, or spin my body off balance. What was the secret of these old men who were so vigorous and strong? Masters of the martial arts retained their vigor into the eighties and nineties, then, almost without exception, they died, quietly and with dignity. Whatever it was, it was certainly more than physical exercise. They practised "moving meditation." They could stop, empty themselves of fears and stresses, become strong, become gentle.

11. Erich Fromm. *The Sane Society*, p. 175.
12. ·Ginseng was introduced to European countries some 270 years ago. Since that time, many European researchers, especially in Germany, Russia, Bulgaria, France, England, and Switzerland have taken special interest in ginseng. They, any more than Eastern researchers, have been unsuccessful in finding the key to its unusual powers.
13. A more homely example can be drawn from the onion. This vegetable has skin over skin, which must be peeled away if one wants to get to the core. So, too, the core of the martial arts may be reached only by peeling away layer upon layer of superficial difficulties. The removal of each layer only reveals a new challenge. It would be foolish to conclude that an onion is nothing but skin, to be discarded as worthless. It were equally foolish to say that the martial arts are nothing but layers of sport (wrestling, boxing, fencing) or entertainment (breaking boards and concrete with one's finger or forehead).
14. Neil Armstrong's words as his foot touched the moon's surface were: One small step for me: a giant leap for mankind.
15. "Weakness" is a relative term. One will never totally overcome human limitations; but these limitations are not "evil." They are useful in that they produce the tension necessary to rally action in the other direction.
16. The example of Watergate is a grim reminder of how political ambition can get out of hand, to the corruption of many.
17. Aristotle. *Nichomachean Ethics*, iv, 3.

Chapter **3**

THE MARTIAL ARTS AND RELIGION

Under heaven nothing is more soft and yielding than water.
Yet for attacking the solid and strong, nothing is better.
It has no equal.
The weak can overcome the strong;
The supple can overcome the stiff.

Tao Te Ching

If there be righteousness in the heart,
*   there will be beauty in the character.*
If there be beauty in the character,
*   there will be harmony in the home.*
If there be harmony in the home,
*   there will be order in the nation.*
If there be order in the nation,
*   there will be peace in the world.*

Confucius

I

The individual who desires to live fully in the way of the oriental martial arts, in contrast to one who superficially practises only physical skills, must attain such a level of self-discipline as will merge his conscious mind with the very principle of life itself. When the martial artist achieves this state of "no-mind" he will find himself invincible, for he will be in a state of at-one-ment with the all-powerful being that is beyond life and death. At this level the martial artist displays to those who see him a seeming contradiction, being simultaneously conscious and unconscious. This is the highest level of his art.

Martial art is, in one sense, a spiritual practice whose object is the ideal self, whose salvation is achieved by emptying the mind of all base desire. Today, as in every age, people are desperately in search of something to believe in. Materialism has always left man hollow; politicians have betrayed their elector's confidence; many persons experience the heartbreak of broken homes and loss of faith in God. How does one cope with life's endless frustrations?

According to Schopenhauer, life is "a curse of endless craving and endless unhappiness." Bertrand Russell, a contemporary philosopher, states: "We stand on the shore of the ocean, crying for the night and the emptiness." Thus, in Western philosophy, for those who do not believe in God, life appears to be unhappy, miserable, even hopeless.

But there is another side to the picture. Life's meaning is directly related to one's positive perception of the nature of the eternal (conveniently designated by the term, God). For Socrates God was the daimon, or inner voice. Accordingly, there can be no happiness in life greater than communion with God, the creator of the universe. For Emmanuel Kant, this was the Christian God. "As I go outside and behold the sky," he said, "I am stirred at the greatness of God."

For the Christian, the Bible is the base for dogma and morals, the Judeo-Christian ethical tradition. This tradition rests on the belief in the supernatural; ethical distinctions are set forth on the foundation of God's word. God is not only a subject for philosophers, but is a theological reality and the ultimate answer to the riddle of life. That He is a moving power in the affairs of men cannot be doubted when one reads history. Thus, Albert Einstein moved from his position as a staunch atheist to his conviction of faith in a Creator. "I cannot believe that God would choose to play dice with the world."

The Christian God is, above all, providential and personal. In the end even Napoleon, who had for most of his life spurned faith, conceded to Christ. "I know men," he said, "and I tell you, Jesus is more than a man. Comparison is impossible between him and any other human being who ever lived." Buddha and Confucius were great men and founders of world religions, but were they God? The difference is sounded by C.S. Lewis, one-time skeptic and professor at both Oxford and Cambridge Universities:

> A man who was merely a man and said the sort of things Jesus
> said wouldn't be a great moral teacher. He would either be a
> lunatic, on the level with a man who says he's a poached
> egg—or else he would be the devil of hell; you must take your
> choice. Either this was and is the Son of God, or else a made
> man, or something worse. You can shut Him up for a demon; or
> you can fall at his feet and call Him Lord and God. But don't
> come up with any patronizing nonsense about his being a great
> moral teacher. He hasn't left that alternative open to us.[1]

When the martial arts make reference to religion, it is in an eclectic sense. That is, the arts can and do exist within the tenets of any and all world religions. Lao-tzu, Confucius, and Buddha were all born long before Christ. Taoism, Confucianism, Buddhism, and Hinduism were well established by the time Christ was born. Mohammedanism (Islam) began and grew from the sixth century on. The martial arts, in some form, were in vogue since the beginning of civilization. Religious ideas were incorporated into the art as they provided a spiritual and psychological foundation for attitudes and practices inherent in its full play.

The martial arts without spiritual foundation are like a face without eyes, for all men have both spiritual and physical needs. It is a mistake to think of any martial art as consisting in a collection of technical routines organized around certain rules of physical movement. The chief aim of the martial artist is to find and develop the common ground between human nature and external nature. Understanding the essentiality of spirit comprises an integral ingredient in achieving perfection in the martial arts.

II

Because the martial arts as a form of unarmed combat originated in East Asia, they were greatly influenced by East Asian religions. Consequently, a brief look at these religions is in place here.

Eastern religions began with a basic reverence for nature of which the gods (or God) form a part. In contrast to Western Christianity which holds reward in the afterlife as a prime motivation for behavior, Oriental belief looks for happiness in this life. Aristotle's "golden mean" was already embodied in the tension-of-opposites symbolized by the familiar yin-yang picture of two fish placed in a circle, head to tail, one white with a black eye, the other black with a white eye. Yin represents the feminine; it dominates at birth and death, is passive and receptive, is "night" (cool, dark, less active), and "winter" (cold, reserved). Yang represents the masculine; it dominates during one's life, is outgoing and stronger, is "day" (warm, energetic), and summer (hot, extroverted). In scientific terms, yin is acid (potassium), sugar; yang is alkaline (sodium), salt.[2]

Yin-yang polarity is not to be interpreted as the principle of evil opposing the principle of good. If it were, a person would strive to eliminate the evil and promote the good. More truly, this polarity is complementary as male complements female, shade light, west east. Male, shade, and west are not "bad" for female, light, and east; they only show different facets of an entity. They complete each other. Yin and yang are two poles of the same cosmic force.

> The ideograms indicate the sunny and shady sides of a
> hill...The art of life is not seen as holding to yang and
> banishing yin, but as keeping the two in balance because there
> cannot be one without the other.[3]

This simple but profound belief paved the way for Taoism, Confucianism, and later, Buddhism.

Tao is introduced and defined as the Way, the principle, cosmic order, nature. Lao-tzu, its founder, maintained that Tao cannot be defined. "The Tao that can be expressed in words," he said, "is not the eternal Tao." The Tao is vague and eluding, deep and obscure, but it does contain form and essence. Its standard is the natural. In the natural order human beings are not treated as special creatures. In fact, human values are regarded as negative forces in the great chain of the natural order.

> The Way brings forth,
> Its virtue fosters them,
> With matter they take shape,
> And circumstance perfects them all;
> That is why all things
> Do honor the Way
> And venerate its power...
>
> So when the Way brings forth,
> Its power fosters all:
> They grow, are reared,
> And fed and housed until
> They come to ripe maturity.[4]

Since language is incapable of conveying a precise definition of Tao—"those who know the Tao do not speak of it; those who speak of it do not know it"—one must seek its relationship to the martial arts in another way. The martial artist searches for Tao in contemplative action and in active contemplation; that is, in the cultivation and refinement of mind and body together.

Taoism teaches that the best way to live is in accordance with nature. One can be truly free only when liberated from all artificial restraints. Attachment to something means a form of identification with it; to the degree one is "attached" by desire or possession, to that degree one is it. Fears, sufferings and problems are the result of un-natural living. Taoism, the way of the uninhibited, insists on naturalness, spontaneity, and simplicity. One keeps oneself in a state of receptivity like the limpid surface of a still body of water.

> As the soft cleave of the water cleaves obstinate stone,
> So to yield with life solves the insoluble:
> To yield, I have learned, is to come back again.

> But this unworded lesson
> This easy example,
> Is lost upon men.
> Man at his best, like water,
> Serves as he goes along:
> Like water, he seeks his own level,
> The common level of life,
> Loves living close to the earth,
> Living clear down in his heart,
> Loves kinship with his neighbors,
> The pick of words that tell the truth.[5]

The martial arts function, as does Tao, with nature. The more one understands Tao, the more one's art is refined and sublimated. When Tao is practised to an equal degree by, say, a Zen Buddhist and a swordsman, there is no way of determining the superiority of one over the other. That is to say, there are many ways of searching for perfection: some do it through painting and music, others through drama, philosophy or religion, still others through the martial arts. The heroes in each field share Tao in an equal degree if each experiences the state of void where the self and the universe are one. In the "void" virtue is revealed.

When only the technique of Tao is practised, it is impermanent and inferior. It is told that when the swordsman Musashi, who had been victorious in sixty duels, faced Takuango, a Zen Buddhist, Musashi lost because he lacked inner depth. After the fight, Musashi shut himself off in a corner of the temple where he devoted himself to deep meditation and a consideration of classical teachings. This so improved his style that he became known as "the saint of the sword."

As in Tao, the spirit of the martial arts cannot be taught. Only technique can be taught. While it is relatively easy to learn several techniques of any martial art, it is impossible to grasp the genuine spirit of the art unless one laboriously works it out for oneself. No master of the martial arts can teach that spirit of the art which has been nurtured in the long stream of Oriental thought. If one takes Oriental thought to be the subject of mere curiosity, and takes the martial arts, the highly refined product of these thoughts, to be a passing titillation, he is very badly off base.

III

While Taosim upholds the cessation of striving, the result only of the illusion of desire, Confucianism looks to the practical side of life. Certain tenets are common to both religions: the belief in the innate goodness of man, the working with nature, reverence for ancestors, and the idea of opposites in tension (yin-yang). However, the rise of Confucianism was sparked by the need for bringing order out of chaos in government, society, and the individual. Thus, the stress is on practicality, outlined in the *Wu-Ching* (of which *I Ching* is a part) and the Ssu Shu (of which the *Analects* are an important section). A systematic hierarchy of rank was organized in which the lower deferred to the higher rank (son to father, wife to husband, subject to ruler, and so on). To ensure the continuity and solidarity of this relationship, rituals and ceremonies became a vital feature. Individuals are to strive for the virtues of *chi* (wisdom), *li* (propriety), *hsin* (honesty), and most of all *jen* (compassion).

The establishment of a hierarchy suggests belief in a class structure. Confucian "class," however, did not come through the accident of birth or wealth; one earned it by excelling in virture through energetic effort and innate wisdom.[6]

This coincides perfectly with a basic principle of the martial arts: one achieves mastership by action rooted in contemplation, not by the vulgar display of medals and certificates. This combines the best in both Taoism and Confucianism. Whereas Tao asks that one practise virtue quietly and naturally, Confucianism urges a realistic and active involvement in society. The martial arts preserve the continuity of tradition while adapting to advances and improvements in the present. Confucian politics retained many of the old rituals and diplomatic formalities, being grounded in the moral responsibility of the ruler for the welfare of the governed. Confucius did not say that many could be happy only in society, but that man's nature is best fulfilled in the company of other human beings. This is the ideal that the martial arts likewise favor. "The man of *jen*," say the *Analects*, "is one who, desiring to develop himself, develops others, and in desiring to sustain himself, sustains others. To be able from one's own self to draw a parallel treatment of others: that may be called the way to practise *jen*."[7] This is really the Tao interpreted by Confucianism. It is likewise the basis for the martial arts as they provide for right action, described in the five basic social relationships of Confucian ethics. The subordinate must obey and remain loyal to his superior, but it is also his duty to advise his superior to the right course of action, as he sees it. Just so is the link between student and master in the martial arts.

> In the way of the superior man there are four things, to none
> of which I have as yet attained—to serve my father as I would
> require my son to serve me; to serve my prince as I would re-
> quire my minister to serve me; to serve my elder brother as I
> would require my younger brother to serve me; and to offer
> first to my friends what one requires of them.[8]

IV

Both Taoism and Confucianism were challenged by the introduction of Buddhism from India early in the second century A.D.[9] The two major sections of Buddhism today are probably the Mahayana and the Hinayana, distinguished by the degree of strictness that the rules are kept. The word *yana* means a small craft which carries the followers over the sea of life to the quiet shores of Nirvana.[10]

Buddha himself denied the existence of God of gods, and certainly never insisted on his own godship. Buddha's teachings are not based on inspired revelation but on a rational, moral consciousness. All things, animate and inanimate, human and sacred, are transitory, mere passing scenes in the moving picture of life. Therefore, it is foolish to become attached to anything.

Nirvana, the state of absolute release from existence, is the goal one strives to reach. To attain this state, desires and passions must be suppressed, personality must be entirely subordinated. All virtues are important, but the greatest is benevolence.

The martial arts do not accept the negative aspects of total extinction of personality and non-existence among these beliefs. They embrace the positive precepts of physical discipline and self-reliance. These are attained through the practice of the eight-fold path of right aims, good conduct, knowledge, effort, speech, meditation, livelihood, and mindfulness to Nirvana (heaven on earth), the perfect earth where each soul merges with the whole of nature.

> *Now, after two years of training, it no longer seemed incongruous that such a deadly (martial) art should have largely sprung from ancient temples, mostly Chinese, thence to be modified by men who were among the finest philosophers of their time.* [11]

Of the many different schools of Buddhism that developed in China, Japan, and Korea, the most relevant to the martial arts is Ch'an (Chinese), Zen (Japanese), or Sun (Korean), transliterations of the Sanskrit *dyana*, a kind of meditation that leads to tranquility. Zen is probably the most written about in the West. It is a way of seeing and knowing by looking into one's own nature. Truth comes through active meditation; enlightenment is both sudden and intuitive. The Zen master facilitates the moment of enlightenment by referring directly to some natural, commonplace matter. The main qualities of this moment are irrationality, intuitive insight, authoritativeness, affirmation, a sense of the beyond, an impersonal mood, a feeling of exaltation, and momentariness.

From Buddhism the martial arts adopt the feature that meditation and action are one. Achievement of the goal involves contemplation of those actions that are directly poured out from the inner region undimmed by intellect. It is this method which is emphasized in Japan, especially by the samurai, who, although they had no use for the pacifism (*ahimsa*) of the Buddha, did enjoy the cultivation of stern discipline and spontanieity, of perfect self-control coupled with enormous verve.

Anyone who has read the *Tao-Te-Ching* or *Chuang-tze*, as well as Zen cannot help but note that Zen owes much more to Taoism than to Buddhism. Arthur Wright makes this point:

> *The distrust of words, the rich store of concrete metaphor and analogy, the love of paradox, the bibliophobia, the belief in*

*direct, person-to-person, and often wordless communication
of insight, the feeling that life led in close communion with
nature is conducive to enlightenment—all these are colored
with Taoism.* [12]

It was Lao-tzu, and not Buddha, who said:

*He who knows does not speak;
He who speaks does not know.*

Taoism goes beyond Buddhism. Its most important principle, that of
emptiness, is also one of the basic guides for the spiritual training of the
martial artist. He, too, must "cling single-heartedly to interior peace,"
not the peace of the grave, but the peace of harmonious blend of body
and spirit.

The practical application of this state of mind can be seen in the
way a martial artist in action can anticipate his opponent's every move
instinctively, both to block and to retaliate.

*"Ah!...Focus your body when the blow comes, and meet it
with your spirit if you are unable to block..." Naturally, the
best defence against a blow is to avoid it, parry it, or block it.
Yet sometimes a blow is inevitable...In this case, the Karateka
should not merely tense up. He should meet the blow with his
'ki' or spirit. Physically speaking, it seems that just as the blow
reaches the surface of the body and begins to unleash its
power, the body is not hard, but relaxed. Thus the initial part
of the blow is absorbed by relaxed tissues, by softness. Then,
as the blow continues to penetrate, the body becomes iron-
hard, and the blow, already half spent, is repulsed. Strong men
have been injured, in wrist and elbow, while attempting to
strike a person who is able to do this.* [13]

This point of blocking an attack and its instant reprisal or counter-attack
is where the martial artist's consciousness abides. Emphasis on the unconscious brings out the essential concern with active, non-discursive,
intuitive insight. Preparing for "enlightenment" follows the same route
as mastering the martial arts.

Another Taoistic, rather than Buddhist, precept is that softness is
the function of the way. The martial artist shows this in avoidance of
display, not taking unfair advantage of another, and striving rather than
competing. Allowing things to take their natural course is the positive
side of non-action. So-called softness is often the expression of real inner
strength, and in the long run, overcomes brute force.

> *Herein is the subtle wisdom of life:*
> *The soft and weak overcome the hard and strong.*
> *That the weak overcome the strong, and the soft overcomes the hard,*
> *This is something known by all, but practised by none.*[14]

V

Since the martial arts are oriented to the positive, one cannot be satisfied with just avoiding the wrong things. None of the religions considered in this chapter settles for a "thou-shalt-not" mentality. In the East, Buddhism and Taoism appealed to the peasant, the poor, the underdog, while Confucianism, stressing education and advancement, appealed to the upper and scholar classes, growing more and more in urban centers. Orientals are known for their calm acceptance of the Buddhist monk as well as for the fierce fanaticism of the kamikaze pilots.

> *In Japan, Zen was intimately related from the beginning of its history to the life of the samurai. Although it has never actively incited them to carry on their violent profession, it has passively sustained them when they have for whatever reason once entered into it. Zen has sustained them in two ways, morally and philosophically, because it treats life indifferently.*[15]

The *Michigan State News* of December, 1978, carried an account by Shigeo Imamura, then an associate professor at Michigan State University. He had served as a kamikaze pilot thirty-three years earlier, at which time he was prepared to die "in a most honorable way" for his country by nose-diving into an American battleship.

> *I felt 110 percent Japanese; ultranationalism had spread like wildfire and everyone absorbed it. We believed we had to conquer the world for world peace, and everyone went all out for the homeland's mission. Ninety-eight percent of our pilots were getting shot down in the air combat, so we felt we might as well go down in glory instead of maybe in vain.*

The Confucian ethic tends to be negative, as the Tao tends to be passive. The philosophy of the martial arts is, perhaps, more closely akin to the Western (Christian) tradition of moral virtue, which rests on a principle embodying both negative and positive elements. To observe the standards set forth in the Judeo-Christian writings of the Bible and tradition is socially and morally good; to transgress them is evil. The Golden Rule of Confucius, "Do not do to others as you would not have them do to you," is most positively stated in the Christian command: "Love your enemy, do good to those who hate you," and thus overcome evil by good. This intensity pervades the spirit of the martial arts. A slavish performance of outward acts does not constitute virtue either in Christianity, Taoism, or Confucianism. Personal conviction must inspirit every act.

Taoism needs definition, and ends in proclaiming the impossibility of definition. Confucianism re-interprets Tao as an ideal of moral virtue; its maxims, however, are rather inactive because mainly negative. The active principle of the martial arts is, like Christianity, active and passionate. Unlike Christianity which looks for complete and final fulfillment in the afterlife, the martial arts seek self-realization in this life. Buddhist Nirvana is reached once all desire is eliminated. But one cannot be a member of society without being in it. Some desire is inevitable while one lives—at least the desire to live is there, or one would die. The task of the martial artist is to be in control of desire. Only through the practice of virtue, in the discipline of doing what is right and natural, can one achieve perfection. Human limitation is a bond that the martial artist takes in stride; by daring to train his sights on perfection, despite such limitation, he enlarges the boundaries of human activity and specifically benefits not only himself but all mankind.

NOTES TO CHAPTER 3

The first epigram is quoted from *The Beginner's Guide to Kung-Fu* by Felix Dennis and Paul Simmons. This book has no page numbers. The second epigram is quoted from *The Religions of Man* by Huston Smith, p. 169.

1. Jim Cotter, from "Jesus and the Philosopher," in a campus lecture, not published.
2. William Logan and Herman Petras, *Handbook of the Martial Arts and Self Defense* (Funk and Wagnalls, New York, 1975), p. 271.
3. Alan Watts, *Tao: the Watercourse Way* (Pantheon Books, New York, 1975), p. 21.
4. Lao-tzu, *Tao Te Ching*, 51, trans. R.B. Blakeney (New American Library, New York, 1955), p. 104.
5. *The Jatakata*, as quoted in *The Wisdom of Buddha* (The Philosophical Library, New York, 1968), pp. 29-30.
6. Napoleon's principle for promotion in the army suggests the same idea: the tools to him who can use them.
7. *The Analects*, 20, XI-XIII.
8. B.S. Consall, *Confucianism and Taoism* (The Epworth Press, London, 1934), p. 123.

NOTES TO CHAPTER 3

9. Comprehensively, others should be included—Shintoism, Hindiusm, Jainism, Sikh Movements, to name just a few—but this would take the subject of martial arts too far afield. The connections between the various disciplines can easily be made by the individual reader.

10. Buddhism has some interesting parallels with Western Christian beliefs. The image of the boat is one. In Christian symbolism, the boat is the church, St. Peter and his successors the helmsmen. In Buddhist history, Gautama's mother was supposed to have been born of a miraculously impregnated virgin, like to the virgin birth of Jesus. Like the resurrection and ascension of Christ, Buddha also reach ecstasy, ascending from first, to second, to third, and finally to outer space.

11. C.W. Nicol, *Moving Zen* (William Morrow and Co., New York, 1975), p. 127.

12. Arthur F. Wright, *Buddhism in Chinese History* (Stanford University Press, Stanford, 1959), p. 67.

13. C.W. Nicol, *op. cit.*, p. 126 ff.

14. *Tao Te Ching*, 76-77.

15. D.T. Suzuki, *Mysticism* (Harper, New York, 1957), p. 89.

Chapter **4**

THE MARTIAL ARTS: BEGINNINGS

Flower in the crannied wall,
I pluck you out of the crannies,
I hold you here, root and all, in my hand,
Little flower—but if I could understand
What you are, root and all, and all in all,
I should know what God and man is.
                    —Alfred Lord Tennyson

The tree that does not bend with the wind
will be broken by the wind.
                    —Zen saying

There is no need to make the case for martial arts. They have existed from the beginning, if for no other reason than for human survival. Today the arts have many varieties of form, school, and name, designating goals, and methods of achieving them. Beyond the great number of these arts is the individuality inherent in their proper practice. Every practitioner works out the style and method unique to him, as each person's capacities, attitudes, needs and training are unlike anyone else's.

It would be quite impossible to provide a comprehensive catalogue of the martial arts in all their forms, but some study of them is imperative in order to gain an appreciation of their present state and development. Therefore, this chapter will look briefly at a form popularized by cinema and television. Then will follow a more detailed history, comparison and contrast of two other major schools of the martial arts.

I

Deep secrecy surrounded the beginnings of many martial arts, first as a matter of pride, and then as a matter of safety. No artist wanted his hard-earned successes to be cheapened by superficial imitations, nor did he want to be threatened by his own "weapons" improved on by another. Therefore, he was cautiously selective in whom he admitted as a student or disciple, even within his own family. Many a master let his skills die with him rather than expose them to an unworthy inheritor.

As for safety, many rulers banned the practice of martial arts, for they posed a threat to imperial power. Hence, secret societies became rampant, many of them strong.[1] Yet, there were times when rulers who had banned them called on the superior discipline and skill of martial artists to defend the country against invaders. The story is told of an emperor calling on unarmed monks to repel seemingly insuperable forces that threatened the kingdom. The monks did indeed save the kingdom, but their victory cost them dearly. Having survived the armed attack of foes, the monks fell victim to the emperor's treachery. He had them all put to death, as their valor and strength were now seen as a threat to the emperor.

Kung-fu enjoyed an upsurge of popularity because of the movies made by Bruce Lee (who died in 1973 at the age of 33). Though the movies called his art kung-fu, Lee adapted, modified, and refined many features of other schools outside the kung-fu style, such as karate and tae kwon do. In fact, because certain routines considered essential to kung-fu did not please *him*, Lee disregarded them, to the chagrin of kung-fu purists.

Hua To is the name most often used in designating the founder of kung-fu. The art began supposedly around 300 A.D. in the time of the Chinese warlords, bandits, and secret societies. True to Tao teachings, Hua To's desire to bring Buddhist monks close to nature influenced the types of exercises he devised for this art. To bear arms was forbidden; yet, one needed a means of defense against roaming bandits who often attacked and looted indiscrimately and without warning. Buddhist monks began coupling physical routines with their prayer routines, for monasteries became a prime target for plunder. Self-defense became a matter of life or death. Military leaders added more aggressive routines, and so the combination of the monks' philosophical emphasis and the military's physical force became the basis for what is known today as kung-fu.

Like any genuine art, kung-fu (known as tai chi chuan to some), also stresses the co-ordination of mind and body. It is to be used not only as a means of self-defense, but as a way of right living, physically and spiritually. *What* one does is not as important as *how* and *why* one does it. The superior artist frowns on any form of excess. He looks to nature for his models.[2]

The animal world in particular serves as guide. The movements of insects, birds, and beasts of prey are carefully studied and imitated. Even motivation can be learned from the animals, which act naturally. They never attack, for instance, without provocation or need. Hence, neither does a practitioner of the martial arts act only because he is angry, irritated, or boastful. To do so is unnatural and harmful. The perpetrator of unnatural deeds, whether man or beast, has gone berserk, and must be stopped for his own safety and that of others. Brute force without mind and heart is worse than useless: it is tragic. Prudence must disarm excess.

Thus, tai chi chuan (or kung-fu), initially practised for health, was eventually influenced by Taoist meditative-respiratory techniques which later became an integral part of the art. Still later, efforts to make tai chi chuan a sport met with little success. Since unrestricted contests are no longer permitted, solo performance makes up the major competitions. Hence, the function of kung-fu, other than as training for tournaments and as a base for Chinese opera and acrobatics, is largely found in self-defense and physical culture.

Whatever the reputation of the military, the spirit of the Chinese martial arts is alive and well. A verse from Ch'u Yuan (332-295 B.C.) reflects this:

> ...their limbs were torn,
> Their hearts could not be repressed;
> They were more than brave:
> They were inspired with the spirit of martial art.

II

Buddha's *charity,* Lao-tzu's *humility,* and Confucius' *humanity* teach that the secret of self-defense lies in the effective "way" of self-attack, even of self-denial. This is the "way of the warrior" as embodied in Korean hwarang-do, and in Japanese bushido, the codes of behavior and morals locked into the origins and military history of the two nations. Though mutually dependent in origin and development, each evolved in its own way into a pattern governing warriors in battle.

From vague beginnings in the early Japanese feudal and pre-feudal periods, the creed of bushido served until the seventeenth century as an accepted moral guide, rule of life, and set of ideals for the Samurai or military class.

The early political life of Japan was organized around a clan system. Toward the beginning of the Christian era, there existed a number of clans in central and western Japan, each tracing its descent from a common ancestor, the members bearing the same surname, and each presided over by a highpriest or priestess. The clan institution was thus characterized by a spirit of brotherhood, and the seed of bushido flourished in this atmosphere of cooperative responsibility for the protection and security of the clan.

One of these clans lived in the Yamato Plain just south of the present-day city of Kyoto in central Honshu. The Yamato clan prospered and expanded until, by the third or fourth century A.D., it was the dominant clan in central and western Japan. The highpriest of the clan assumed first place among the other clan chiefs and the worship of the sun goddess became an integral part of the other clans' regimen. A descendant of the highpriest of the Yamato clan reigns today as Hirohito, Emperor of Japan, and the sun goddess remains the primary Japanese deity as symbolized in Japan's flag.

From the late sixth century to early in the ninth century, a period during which the clans possessed a large measure of autonomy, Japan borrowed heavily from the magnificent civilization of China, through Korea. The highpriests of the Yamato clan carried samples of this culture, including Chinese feudalism, from Paekche to Japan. At the time, the chiefs of the imperial Yamato clan ruled more through their prestige and as mediators among the clans, balancing one against the other, than through their own economic and military strength. Thus, from the ninth to the twelfth centuries, the emperor's power declined until he was, in effect, a puppet in the hands of his nobles and their allied provincial aristocrats.

On the one hand, the outside world posed no threat to the authority of the emperor since the aristocrats lacked motivation, simply feeling a mutual animosity. On the other hand, the ministerial offices of the central administration became hereditary and the lands of the great court families and monasteries were exempt from taxation. As the amount of tax-free land increased, heavier taxes were imposed on the remaining land, forcing the owners to cede their property to the holders of the tax-free estates. This increased wealth and power strengthened both the great court families and the monasteries, a situation which led to the formation, prior to the kamakura Shogunate (1185), of a military class supported by the tax-free manorial estates. The Shogunate then initiated a feudal type of military government, uniquely Japanese in character.

The period from the twelfth to the nineteenth century is consequently known as the Feudal Period, the Shogunate military system being feudalistic in the sense that the right to govern was seen as a property right which belonged to anyone with a manor or a fief. The military, social, and political relations between the lords and the shogun, and lords and those who populated their domains, were feudalistic. While the lords were obliged to give loyal and obedient service to the shogun in return for their fiefs and domains, those who lived in the lords' domains owed them loyal and obedient service in return for protection and livelihood.

Bushido appeared during the Ashikaga Shogunate (1333-1568), a period marked by increased fighting among the military in the provinces. It matured during the Tokugawa Shogunate which continued until the nineteenth century. Although, like Korea's hwarang-do, Japanese bushido gradually evolved into a pattern of behavior which governed soldiers under the stress of war, and served as a social guide and rule of life, it developed out of the intimate contractual relationship between the early landholders and their armed retainers, not between friends. Bushido eventually developed into what is today recognized as the spiritual backbone of Japanese martial arts.

III

The history of bushido as related to Japan's development is in strong contrast to that of the hwarang-do and its part in the rise of Korea. From 57 B.C. to 676 A.D. Korea had been divided into the three kingdoms of Koguryu, Paekche, and Silla. Initially the largest and most powerful of the three, Koguryu occupied the entire territory of Manchuria as well as the northern part of the Korean peninsula. Koguryu was especially strong during the fifth century under two of its greatest rulers, both of whom successfully forced Paekche to move its capital to the south. Silla, however, the smallest and considered to be the most vulnerable, was never taken. Though hard pressed, especially near the end of the fifth century, Silla was able to consolidate its people, re-organize its government, and develop institutions to meet the challenge of the times.

Foremost among these institutions was the hwarang, at first a group of aristocratic young men and women, gifted by birth and ability, who were imbued with a sense of mission and a deep desire to protect communal interests through cultivation of mind and body. The hwarang so advanced as to become the vanguard on the battlefield. Their training and courageous leadership produced the generals, statesmen, and kings who were to turn the tide and expand Silla's power. They were committed by loyalty and vision far ahead of their times.

So it was that, compared to Japan, Korea had remained a relatively peaceful nation, "the land of morning calm," under the strong leadership of kings with a powerful central government. Since there were no serious power struggles among the lords, the hwarangdo developed from the "way of the warrior" into a cultural and intellectual code for the sons and daughters of the nobility. During the period of United Silla (661-935), the hwarang entered an era of peace, prosperity, and cultural development with the invention of moveable type (200 years before Gutenberg!). It became a profoundly Buddhist country, printing lengthy Buddhist scriptures and constructing countless Buddhist temples and sculptures throughout the country. At the same time, Silla enjoyed close relations with the flourishing culture of China, particularly Confucianism and Taoism.

While it is true that this period of great prosperity was made possible in large part by the dedicated spirit of the hwarangdo, it is also true that the "way of the warrior" as an aggressive force had a limited place in a period of such enlightened rule. The martial arts did, however, continue to enjoy great prestige, functioning as a regular feature of state festivals and athletic competitions, as part of the education of the young, and in the training of the military. Unfortunately, however, the kings, noblemen, and their children gradually became corrupt, the mighty spirit of the hwarang degenerated, and the hwarang itself appeared decadent. These forces resulted in a breakdown of the communal spirit and an inevitable transfer of power.

While the Koryo dynasty was able to survive for almost five hundred years (918-1391), it was a period of ceaseless struggle against innumerable invasions from the north, including the Sung, Won, and Ming dynasties of China, as well as raids from the south by Japanese pirates. From the beginning of the thirteenth century the Mongol invasions proved to be the most savage and were ultimately fatal; the Mongols were the fiercest and most powerful military force of the then-known world. As soldiers, they were utterly without mercy, putting entire populations to the sword and leveling whole cities to provide pasture-lands for their herds.

In spite of this, however, it was remarkable that although few legitimate successors of the hwarang remained in the military class, those military leaders did protect the king and made it possible for the court to remain on Khanghwa Island for one generation, without yielding to compromise of any sort. Again and again they resisted the most savage brutality, preferring to resist and die rather than to submit to a life of dishonor under the rapacious Mongols. Resist and die they did, but the spirit of hwarangdo survived.

The Buddhist dynasty in Korea was finally brought to an end by Yi Songgye, a great leader and general who was able to suppress the pirates and defeat the raiding Manchus along the northern frontier, as well as to consolidate the country behind him. With the establishment of the Yi dynasty came a system of thorough land reform, as Yi secured the loyalty and service of every element of the population and made provisions for those who had served their country well. However, he simply replaced the Buddhism of the Koryo dynasty with Confucianism, and, instead of a revival of the practice of hwarangdo, his became a leisure dynasty in which only a few sophisticated Confucians enjoyed fruitless discussions, abused their power, and disregarded the constant threat of invasion of Japan and China. During the entire Yi dynasty there lived, it seemed, only one true hwarang: Yi Soonshin. He alone struggled for the hwarang spirit, but he died a lonely death.

Much as Korea desired simply to be left in peace, it was drawn more and more into world affairs until, in 1876, the Yi dynasty opened some ports to Japanese traders. This was followed in 1882 by a treaty with the United States which provided even more outlets for trade. But the last king of Korea was forced by the Japanese to abdicate. This rule lasted until Japan's defeat in World War II. During this period the spirit of hwarangdo emerged in resistance and national defense. It was at this point, too, that the Confucian disapproval of, and lack of support for the military was most bitterly felt. For Korea, with a population of twelve million, had a standing army of only six thousand with which to confront the Japanese who were equipped with modern weaponry and a modernized version of bushido.

From the standpoint of the "way of the warrior," the Japanese annexation of Korea appeared to be, literally, the result of the defeat of hwarangdo by bushido. This was not actually so, however, since the Japanese surrender to the Allied forces certainly illustrated the limitation of bushido's spiritual power. The Korean and Vietnamese wars mark the rebirth of hwarangdo, in its proper sense, in the great martial art of tae kwon do.

IV

The philosophical foundations of both hwarangdo and bushido are common in that they were born of an Oriental culture characterized by Confucianism, Taoism, and Buddhism. Their differences correspond to the differences between the two cultures. While in Korea the three main currents of Oriental thought were not significantly modified as they were assimilated into the national character, in Japan the three original sources were modified to meet the needs of national strength and unification. They were eventually reformulated to enrich the unique religion of Japan as already established in Shinto.

In addition, bushido incorporated elements of Confucianism and Zen Buddhism. From Confucianism it borrowed the concept of loyalty of subordinate to superior in social and family relations (the "Five Relationships"). The son owed loyalty to his father, the younger brother to the elder, the subject to his lord, the wife to her husband, the friend to the friend. According to the Japanese, however, the loyalty of vassal to lord transcended all other loyalties. This duty was passed from father to son, from generation to generation. For example, if the lord's son were threatened by an assassin, it was considered highly ethical for a father to substitute his own son. A theme often found in Japanese tragedy is this struggle between conflicting loyalties.

From Zen Buddhism bushido incorporated the concept that enlightenment is achieved only through one's inward effort, a teaching that led to self-discipline, self-control, and self-conquest. Specifically from Shinto, bushido inherited its strong attachment to the land of Japan and to everything it symbolized. This illustrates how, from earliest times, Japanese rulers used religion to serve political ends. While the Yamato ruler fostered belief in the superiority of their divine ancestress, Amaterasu, in order to justify their assumption of the rulership of all Japan, the Kokugawa rulers stressed Buddhism because it upheld their policies of maintaining the Japanese social and political structure.

The life of bushido's leading philosopher, Yamaga Soko, illustrates that philosophy was indeed the tool of politics. As Japan's foremost thinker in the formulation of bushido, Yamaga Soko was celebrated in Japanese history for his intellectual prowess and fiercely independent mind. Concerned about the prolonged inactivity of the warrior class under the peaceful Tokugawa rule, he believed that the samurai had a more important function to perform than just to keep themselves fit for possible military service. The samurai were provided with a stipend by their lord so that they could enjoy a parasitic existence at the expense of the other social classes, eating the food of the peasant and using the goods of the artisan and merchant. They were so maintained in order to have the freedom to cultivate those arts and virtues which would make them exemplary leaders. Above all, the samurai were to set a high example of devotion to duty. Since duty required the other classes to perform their respective function conscientiously, it should also require the samurai to serve their lords with utmost loyalty and to put moral principles before personal gain.

It was Yamaga who systematized the qualities long honored in Japanese feudal tradition, those qualities necessary to achieve the high ideals of austerity, temperance, constant self-discipline, and a readiness to meet death at any time. It is his life which symbolizes the conversion of the samurai class from a purely military aristocracy to one of increasing political and intellectual leadership. This trend helps to explain why the samurai, instead of becoming an idle and effete class which relied solely on its hereditary privileges, came to serve as the brains of the Restoration Movement, to take the initiative in dismantling feudalism, and to play an important role in Japan's subsequent modernization.

Confucianism was for Yamaga a tool for political utility, for as a theory it had neither meaning nor value unless it generated national unity and political stability. Tokugawa's Buddhism was replaced by Shintoism because the former lacked political relevance. The samurai who overthrew the Tokugawan rulers and replaced Buddhism with Shintoism used this ancient religion to justify their right to rule. Such is utilitarianism!

Thus, Yamaga's intellectual interests did not exactly conform to the Confucian pattern of civil arts and peaceful pursuits. On the one hand, his intense concern for military science led him to devote much time to the study of military strategy and tactics, weapons, and intelligence procedures. Yet he also stressed moral indoctrination as the essence of bushido. His affirmation of intelligence as one of the martial virtues had important implications. Since he himself focused attention on the need for studying and adopting western weapons and tactics as introduced by the Dutch, his heirs in the nineteenth century, antiforeign as they were, quickly realized the need for "knowing the enemy," and thus for learning more about the West.

In short, the man of action was preferable to the theorist. Confucius, the common-sense sage, was a far more effective guide for the samurai than all the abstract thinkers of later times. The value of Buddhism was limited for the same reason. As Yamaga says in *An Autobiography in Exile:*

> *If we should make our abode under the trees or upon some*
> *rock in lonely solitude, scorning worldly honor and fame, we*
> *might be able to attain to an inexpressible state of unselfish*
> *purity and mystical freedom. But when it comes to the affairs*
> *of the world, of the state, and of the four classes of the people,*
> *needless to say, we should be able to accomplish nothing in*
> *that manner. Even in minor matters, we should have less com-*
> *prehension of things than the uneducated man in the street.*[3]

Yamaga's philosophy stresses utilitarianism and patriotism; action is of the utmost importance:

> *Whatever others may think, I myself cannot believe otherwise*
> *or accept that kind of learning as satisfactory. I have consulted*
> *both Confucians and Buddhists on this question, made inquiry*
> *of persons reputed to be eminent in virtue, and carefully ob-*
> *served their methods and actions, only to find that they are not*
> *in accord with the real world. Their teaching goes one way and*
> *life goes another.*[4]

Yamaga was convinced that Japanese civilization was far superior to Chinese civilization, and that his own nation, not China, was both the center and the zenith of all culture. While in China dynasties had come and gone, and Confucianism had been corrupted almost beyond recognition, the Japanese alone had set an example of unswerving loyalty.[5]

Now, hwarangdo had fared quite differently from bushido, despite their common roots. Hwarangdo was able to select carefully the best of each of the major religious beliefs and combine the secular with the sacred. From Confucianism, for example, the hwarang adopted the teachings of filial piety, loyalty to state, and empathy toward one's fellow man; from Taoism they adopted a seemingly paradoxical method of managing affairs (i.e., the doctrine of action by non-action, the teaching of communication by non-discourse); and from the teachings of Buddha they accepted the commitment to reject evil and effectively act for the common good.

Wonkwang, a Buddhist monk, wrote the "Five Secular Commandments" at the request of Kwisan and Chuhang, two hwarangdo warriors who sought advice on the purification of their minds and the regulation of their conduct. These commandments included loyalty to the king, filial piety, sincerity with friends, non-retreat in battle, and rational selectivity in the killing of living beings.[6] In the ranks of the hwarang, only the most positive and permanent elements of their eclectic philosophy were incorporated into the social and cultural fabric of the Korean people.

While Japanese thinkers posited that wisdom must work for the unity of the people and the strength of the state, the Koreans maintained that the state existed to further the welfare of the people by showing the value of morality. This difference in attitude is the key to distinguishing hwarangdo from bushido. Attitude determined the practical application of religious belief. Buddhism, for example, strove for the protection of the state and stressed the self-strength available to those who were able to return to their original purity. Since the battle was one of the means whereby one could free himself from his ego, the warrior was justified in not retreating even to the death, as Wonkwang taught. Likewise, Confucian loyalty to king and state was part of one's filial duty. If all other means of maintaining this loyalty failed, fighting became not only a necessity, but a religious duty. The state was not the ultimate goal of the cultivation of the mind and physique, for, in their own right, religious thought and teaching were valuable in themselves.

Further insights into hwarangdo and bushido can be gained by seeing them in action. Both considered death for a good cause an honor, for honor is preferable to life. However, the deeds of the samurai were often motivated by self-righteousness and a desire to show off excellence in swordsmanship. Miamoto Musashi has already been mentioned as the greatest Kendo master of his time. However, while the courage and honor of the samurai belonged either to themselves or to their lords, the virtue of the hwarang existed for its own sake.

Because the hwarangdo formed, in a sense, the backbone of the nation, its motivating spirit influenced every other social class. Even their enemies acknowledged their excellence, and attempted to emulate it. Kwan-ch'ang's relationship to General Kaebaek, the commander of the Paekche army, is an outstanding example. When Kwan-ch'ang dashed into the enemy camp on horseback and speared several opponents, he was captured and presented to General Kaebaek. When the General removed the warrior's helmet and saw that he was only a boy, he exclaimed, "Alas for us if we cannot match such courage! If these are the deeds of a boy, what must we expect from their men?" In admiration, the general had the boy placed on his horse and returned to his camp. Taking barely enough time to drink a cup of water, the young man repeated his feat and was again captured. This time he was decapitated and his head sent back to the Sillan camp, tied to the saddle of his horse. His father lifted the head, wiped away the blood and proclaimed, "My son's honor lives!" Kwan-ch'ang had been killed not because he was hated, but because he was respected; thus, his life's purpose had been fulfilled, as his honor had been secured.

In contrast, bushido did not emphasize the objective value of virtue, for virtue had to give way to politics and military strategy.[7] The following incident clearly reveals the ruthless determination of the bushido code to crush any power, secular or religious, that stood in its way. This concerns Nobunaga's burning of the Tendai monastery on Mount Hiei. Nobunaga justified his destruction of the venerable center of Japanese Buddhism with its 3000 buildings and 20,000 residents by claiming the need for national law and order. He did not consider his act a result of a vindictive desire to avenge himself on the monks but rather a selfless act of devotion to the cause of unification. In his words:

> I am not the destroyer of the monastery. The destroyer is the
> monastery itself. As you know, I am one who has not known a
> moment's peace. I have risked my life. I have devoted myself
> to hard work and to a life of denial to personal desires. I have
> given myself to the hardships of a warrior's life in order that I
> might restrain the turbulence within the land, check the
> decline of imperial prestige and restore it, improve the prevailing
> manners and customs, and perpetuate the benefits of govern-
> ment and religion. .... It is they who obstruct the maintenance
> of law and order in the country. Those who help the rebels are
> themselves traitors to the country. If, moreover, they are not
> destroyed now, they will again become a peril to the nation.
> Therefore, not a single life should be spared.[8]

In the history of Korea no such leader as Nobunaga is recorded. To destroy cultural heritage in order to achieve political ends is despicable. Culture and virtue always take precedence over utility and expedience; one should give his life only for virtue. Whereas the idea of death in bushido came to be valued as an end in itself, the hwarangdo held that dying for the sake of spectacle is worse than wasted effort: it is vicious self-aggrandizement.

Kongun, who lived during the reign of King Chinp'yong (579-631), was one who suffered just such an unnecessary death, motivated by the erroneous notion that it was more virtuous to die than to expose an act of villainy. During a great famine, when food was strictly rationed, some palace guards stole grain from the government stores and shared it with each other. Kongun, a follower of Hwarang Konrang, knowing of the deed, refused to be associated with it in any way. When he was invited to take a share of the loot, he replied, "As a follower of the hwarang, my mind is cultivated in the garden of wind and moon. Therefore, I refuse to compromise my honor for material wealth. I cannot share what has been wrongfully obtained." The guards not only felt rebuked, but feared exposure; they agreed to plot Kongun's death. He learned of their plan to invite him to a dinner at which he was to be poisoned, but he did nothing to save himself. He reasoned that, since his conscience was clear, he should not be afraid to die; if, on the other hand, he reported the crime, the guards would surely receive the punishment of common thieves, and they were much less prepared for death than he. The historian Kim Pu-sik (1075-1151) had this comment in Sam Kuk Saki:

> Kongun did not die in his place. He died ingloriously for an insignificant matter rather than preserve his life to be used in a matter of consequence.

Life is not be be taken lightly. No one—least of all the hwarang—admires a self-made martyr. For the hwarangdo the only true courage was that which was intelligently controlled within a proper framework of values; one has to scrutinize both the purpose and the results of one's actions.

Another example of bushido's misplaced emphasis on power is the following incident. Musashi,[9] a humble and honest, but headstrong and cruel man, displayed an unusual and questionable code of ethics toward the Yoshiolka clan. He challenged the family to a duel, to which the head of the family responded. Armed with a wooden sword, Musashi first disarmed his opponent, then progressed mercilessly to beat him as he lay on the ground. The noble lord was carried to his home where he cut off his samurai top-knot in shame. When the beaten lord's brother tried to vindicate the family, Musashi fatally crushed his skull with a well-placed blow of his wooden sword. Musashi was then challenged by a pre-teen son of Lord Yoshiolka. Musashi slashed the boy to ribbons and then cut a path through the boy's protectors. This bloody demonstration of Musashi's superior swordsmanship was meaningless, and consequently, dishonorable. Personal revenge holds no place among the hwarangdo.

Hwarangdo confronted bushido during Hideyoshi's Korean expeditions from 1592 to 1597. Nobunaga's legacy to Hideyoshi included the dream of conquering China. While much planning was devoted to achieving maximum efficiency of Japan's naval power and logistic capabilities, it took only Hideyoshi's sudden death to effect the total collapse of this vaunted enterprise and thus illustrate how prematurely Japan had been cast into the role of imperialism. Japan's failure to recognize the existence of Admiral Yi Sunshin, Korea's legitimate heir to the hwarang spirit, was a telling factor in Japan's miscalculation, for he embodied the latent strength of hwarangdo, kept alive in monasteries, estates, and even Confucian colleges scatered throughout the country.

At the time of Japan's invasion, Korea was involved in disputing the interpretation of neo-Confucianism. Refusing to be side-tracked, however, Admiral Yi was able to defeat the larger Japanese fleets, and so prevent supplies from reaching their invading armies.[10] He was entrapped at a crucial moment, and was slandered by political opponents, imprisoned, tortured, and demoted. Despite all this, Yi harbored no resentment. He exemplified by his actions the first commandment of the hwarangdo: to remain loyal to the king even though the king's decision may be faulty. During Yi's imprisonment, his mother died; he was able to pay his filial respects to her only on being freed. He walked several hundred miles in his funeral robe, thus fulfilling the second commandment: filial piety. Yi's successor lost the entire fleet in a disastrous defeat; Yi was re-instated to his command, dutifully accepting an almost impossible task. His only words were written to the king, explaining that, although only twelve battleships remained, he would die the king's able servant. True to the last to the hwarang spirit, he was eventually to give his life in the final battle of Noryang. Through sheer ability (and twelve ships!), Yi annihilated a Japanese fleet of three hundred ships, thereby driving the invaders from the Korean seas and actually ending the war.

One may conclude, that, in their own ways, both bushido and hwarangdo were successful, operating as they did under contrasting principles. Whereas the primary aim of bushido was to kill or be killed, for the hwarangdo it was to win the victory or make one's death useful. Both codes spelled out the "way of the warrior;" being a warrior involved one in battle; battle often meant facing death. Death could be

empty or meaningful, and it was meaningful only if it was virtuous—
that is, spent in a worthy cause.

As bushido remains primarily the embodiment of the Japanese national character, influenced by Shintoism, the product of Japanese
religious practice, hwarangdo belongs to the Korean people only in the
sense that it has been practised by them since the unification of the three
kingdoms. By its very nature, hwarangdo emphasizes widsom over
violence, and remains the ideal not only in Korea but in all countries
honoring this code.

As General Kim Yu-sin, commander during the Sillan unification
of Korea, became the idol of the Korean army, so Admiral Yi Sunshin
remains the model for Korean naval strategists. Tae kwon do, practised
during the period of the three kingdoms, has since become the basic
martial art in the Korean military, not only because it is recognized today as one of the most effective means of self-defense, but because it
developed from the spirit of hwarangdo.

In a similar sense, one cannot discuss Japan's military strength during World War II without considering the nature of bushido. The influence of bushido becomes more obvious when one notes the current
popularity of such works as Musashi's *A Book of Five Rings*. It is written in such a manner that a novice in any walk of life can derive an entire philosophy of life. A samurai can take it even a step further into
death and after-life. Japanese business men, for instance, read
Musashi's book to develop from it what might be termed "the way of
the business man." It goes without saying that to understand Japanese
nationalism and the progress of its prosperity, one should know the
meaning of bushido.

Inasmuch as life is a constant battle in which one is exhorted to
fight the good fight, the martial arts hold a definite place. They proffer
a way of life suited to make the practitioner a person of character and
vitality. The healthy moral advancement of mankind, so often neglected
in the pursuit of technological progress, can both stimulate and be the
result of a proper study and application of the martial arts. The better
world envisioned for the future must be concerned with what is good for
the whole person—mind, body, spirit—and for the whole community
of mankind.

NOTES TO CHAPTER 4

1. Versions of these secret bands are currently described in such novels as *Tai-Pan* and *Shogun*, the latter being made into a popular television series. Modern society contains its own gangland criminals in organized crime. The Mafia and guerilla terrorists are making headlines in our own day. But they are far removed from the aims of martial artists. Black jacket gangs exist illegally for reasons very different from those of the originally outlawed martial arts.

2. Maurice Zalle remarks on the nature of Tai chi chuan:

   Tai chi ch'an is a Chinese system of controlled muscular movement that is both an exercise and a method of self-defense. ... In this system self-protection always takes the form of a reaction to an attack by an aggressor, an attacker.

   Yet the practitioner of this method uses no force in repelling his opponent. His every movement during the bout, the battle, the encounter, is light and soul-like, gentle as a falling leaf.

   In connection with Zen he adds:

   The student of this defensive art must practice these positions statically and dynamically until they become automatic. Then he must enter into Zen if these exercises are to be adequate to protect him from a marauder's onslaught. To enter into Zen, to become a true warrior of any oriental martial art, to obey unconsciously the code of the warrior in the true tradition, one must transcend the principle of body and enter into the world of consciousness.

   Zalle points out that this is true of any martial art.

   He who wishes to live in an oriental martial art, rather than just to practice it on the physical level, must so train his consciousness to attain a self-discipline that at last his conscious mind will merge into an identity with the very principle of life itself.

   See Hu Shih and Chinese Philosophy in *Chan's Essays* (Oriental Society, 1969), compiled by K.H. Chen, p. 294.

3. Yamaga Soko, Sources of Japanese Tradition, Vol. 1, compiled by R. Tsunoda, W.T. De Barry and D. Keene (Columbia University Press, New York, 1958), P. 407.

4. Ibid.

5. In a sense, Yamaga may have been right. This is the case at least of judo, a form of the oriental martial art. The Japanese claim it for their own, but it actually originated in China in a religious order the rules of which forbade the use of weapons, even in self-defense. However, it is important to notice that it was the Japanese who made the present form of judo possible, not merely as a sport but also as a way of life. Not until the late twelfth century did the Japanese learn of the art. Many and varied systems of jujitsu were developed in Japan. In 1882 a Japanese professor, Jigoro Kano, who was familiar with the better of these, set up a system known as judo, which then became the standard. The Japanese managed to keep this a secret for over twenty years, but after the Russo-Japanese War of 1904-1905, it became public, and today most armies, navies, and police forces are taught it. It has even become an event in the Olympic Games. Thus, judo shows how bushido has been internationalized through Japanese effort, and how Chinese abstract philosophies turn out to be a way of life.

6. Ilyon reports the story in his *Samguk Yusa,* or Legends and History of the Three Kingdoms of Ancient Korea, trans. by T.H. Ha and G.K. Mintz (Yonsei University Press, Korea: 1972), p. 286.

   The two men visited the eminent monk and asked him to give them a golden maxim which would serve to guide their behavior through life. Wonkwang replied, "There are ten commandments of the Bodhisattvas, but since you are the subject of a king you can hardly keep them. (That is, these commandments would require them to become monks.) The five secular commandments are: 1) Serve the king with loyalty; 2) Honor your parents with filial piety; 3) Treat friends with sincerity; 4) Fight the

NOTES TO CHAPTER 4

> enemy with bravery; 5) Kill living animals with discriminating mercy. You should observe these commandments consistently, without the least neglect.

7. The characteristics of bushido are well depicted in the method of Zen masters' teaching of bushies. David Suzuki says:

> The soldiers were naturally not very scholarly; what they wanted was to be not timid before death, which they had constantly to face. This was a most practical problem on their part, and Zen was ready to grapple with it, probably because the masters dealt with the facts of life, and not with concepts. ...
>
> They would probably say to the soldier who came to be enlightened on the question of birth and death that, there is no birth and death here; get out of my room as quickly as you can. So saying, they would chase him away with a stick they generally carried. Or if a soldier came to a master saying, "I have to go through at present with the most critical event of life; what shall I do?", the master would roar, "Go straight ahead, and no looking backward!" This was how in feudal Japan the soldiers were trained by Zen masters.

   See D.T. Suzuki, *Zen Buddhism,* ed. by William Barrett (Anchor Books, Longon: 1956), pp. 288-289.

8. Yamaga Soko, Sources of Japanese Tradition, Vol. 1, compiled by R. Tsunoda, W.T. De Barry and D. Keene (Columbia University Press, New York, 1958), P. 315.

9. Jay Gluck in *Zen Combat* (Ballantine Books, New York: 1976), pp. 87-87, describes Miyamoto Musashi (1984-1645) as follows:

> He started his career as the delinquent son of a fencing master, spent much of his adolescence tied to trees or locked in rooms in punishment for some misdemeanor or other. At the age of thirteen, he killed his first man—a rival fencing master who has slighted his father. He came under the tutelage of several of Japan's greatest warrior-priests.
>
> Despite, and partly because of his stormy beginnings he epitomizes "Zen, ken, shu—meditation is the sword, is the brush." His life was one long meditation; detachment from self attained through constant activity; detachment from everyday reality by grappling with it directly, unselfishly. He originated new concepts in fencing, developed the two-sword style, and was never defeated. And with the brush, he stands as one of Japan's greatest painters; in my opinion, the unparalleled master of the sumi-e, simple black ink style.

10. James Scarth Gale, in *History of the Korean People* (Taewon Publishers, Seoul: 1972), pp. 263-264, describes Admiral Yi's "turtle-boat" as "a cleverly-armed vessel."

> It was covered with planks thick and hard. On the top, running lengthwise, was a narrow footway and another ran across. All the rest of the surface was occupied by spikes, spears and blade points. Each boat had a dragon's head carved at the prow for good luck, the mouth fitted with a rude cannon such as the Chinese had long known and made use of. At the rear, underneath the tail, was another porthole for cannon shot. There were six openings on each side, one for a cannon muzzle and the others for the soldiers to shoot through. Sailors, too, had their places down below where they handled the oars. When moving into battle, these boats were covered with light fluff or matting so as not to show their teeth. Any attempt to board them ended in hopeless confusion. Whenever they were surrounded, the guns belched forth fire on all sides. Fearing nothing, they drove straight into the heart of the enemy fleet.

Chapter **5**

THE MARTIAL ARTS AS ARTS OF LIFE

Ours is an open world. We are open not just to the whole world, but to the whole universe. We are on the brink of heaven knows what discoveries out beyond our planet.

If man is around a few more hundred thousand years, there's no telling what he may do. The idea of man mastering his universe in a very fundamental way is not something which we hold as impossible.

—Bernard Cooke

Man's sense of insecurity today has reached unparalleled depths. Victimized by "the system," he has little personal strength left to fall back on, and he finds himself bound to forms and forces over which he has little or no control. Lacking a sense of self that could be sustained despite rejection by the system, modern man also lacks a community of friends who can be counted on to support him regardless of society's misjudgment. Persons no longer are seen as unique individuals, but are too often classified and evaluated by mechanical standards. As cogs in a machine, they are indispensable, disposable, and replaceable, the minute they dare not to adjust smoothly to the rest of the machine.

The martial arts recognize man as part of a dynamic nature. The concrete experiences of life, natural phenomena, and man's awareness of himself in relation to others contain ultimate reality for the martial artist. Man's cosmos includes the potential for a proper appreciation of the divine order of things, the terrible-blissful power that brings all things into existence. In his participation with creation in a vast community of forces, man can realize his own nature and importance by cooperating with the inner necessity of the whole. Thus, when he lives in the fullness of the eternal rhythm, the martial artist realizes his most profound level of awareness. He is, indeed, the artist of life.

The martial artist believes that man obtains knowledge of this eternal rhythm by viewing the patterns of change in both the natural and social worlds. While this rhythm is too mysterious to be confined to any simple conceptual form, man can know it directly if he remains sensitive to its expression, because consciously or unconsciously, he participates in it. This eternal power, as manifested in life's encounters, provides answers to the most perplexing questions of the human condition. The natural rhythms of life are recognized, for instance, in the alternations of day and night, the cycle of the seasons, and the natural relations among people. The conclusion that man passes through sequences of beginnings and endings only to begin again, reflects a view of man's place in the universe quite different from the view that he was completed in an instant, and will remain forever as at that moment.

ın Oriental thought, nature—sun, rivers, mountains, trees—all are "divine;" creation and existence are a never-ending process rather than a *fait accompli*. The process is continuously being spelled out in the dynamics of growth, movement, change, and the re-stabilization of forces in tension. The concern of the martial artist is not so much to learn the revelation of a divine will, as to live out his capacity for spontaneously expressing the natural order and rhythm of life. In these terms, man can be comfortable in this world, without having to wait for the next. He can enjoy the manifestation of divine energy in relation to all things, here and now.

Perhaps the closest expression of the martial artist's philosophy is the "actionless activity" of Taoism. This is achieved through a growing relaxation from artificial conventions of thought and action. Growth and understanding do not consist of an intellectualizing of internal forces, nor do they mean living according to prescribed rules for the sake of rules. They are, rather, the opening of one's life to spontaneous living.

The martial artist, like the Taoist sage, does not interfere with the mutual flow of the Tao. While the means of expressing and fulfilling man's basic needs have changed much and often, the needs themselves have changed little since primitive times. Where physical and biological needs are concerned mainly with procuring food, clothing and shelter, psychological and social needs go to the deeper demands of peer acceptance, a sense of achievement, relative security, and a modicum of happiness. One must have the opportunity to belong, to think, to believe.

All cultures through the ages have held certain views regarding the political, social, economic, and religious forces of their times. Physical exercise, perhaps the oldest form of human education, is one of these forces. Used by different peoples for fitness and for purposes of learning, religion, aesthetics, politics, recreation, and defense, it has remained an integral aspect of a healthy philosophy of life. Where it is eliminated, restrained, or unreasonably subjugated, ills of all sorts result.

A study of the various mores and customs of these cultures reveals the value of physical exercise and the uses to which it has been put. From this, one can analyze and interpret the influences that assorted cultures have had on the methods of exercise, and upon the subsequent development of philosophies of the martial arts. As practised in the Orient, physical exercise is neither merely sport nor the stoic endurance of pain; neither masochism nor sadism has any part in this philosophy.

The art of full living as advocated by the martial arts continually reviews total fitness programs. A total health *concept* must include freedom from disease and defects, a sanitary environment, and the peace of mind to pursue personal actualization. The martial arts in health education promote those attitudes and habits in daily living that bring the greatest good to the greatest number.

In this context, attitude is a key word. It originally meant a suitable bodily posture for a specific activity, or a bodily posture indicating a certain mental state or emotion. Through common usage the word now refers to a persistent mental posture or state of mental readiness, and is commonly associated with personality. It is through consistent response that an individual is able to identify attitude. Obviously, technique plays an important role, as mind-set and practice are mutually reinforcing. Such attitudes as honesty, fair play, cooperation, respect for rules and for one's opponent are essential. The interaction of belief and practice is necessary for the complete development of the individual and of any skills he is to acquire.

An essential to any art is style and skill. The art of life is no exception. Anyone can draw a bow over strings, but only the skilled musician can do so musically. The martial artist carries his training into every facet of life's experiences. So he is poised and confident not only on the gym floor, but also in the way he walks and talks on the street. He applies positive and creative ways of thinking not only to mastering a difficult martial routine, but to the way he treats his family and friends. He considers the how as much as the what, since for him form and matter are inseparable.

How does one measure life? By longevity? By experience? By the kind and depth of passion? Or by a combination of all these? An oyster, protected by its shell and well adapted to the diffuse food contained in the water it draws in, may outlive a cuttlefish, which has superior methods of managing unexpected contingencies, "the sum of vital activities during any given interval" being far greater than in the oyster. So a worm, protected and nourished by the earth, may live longer than an insect, but the insect during its metamorphosis from egg, to larva, to adult may experience much more of what constitutes "life."

The same is true in the human scale. Herbert Spencer points out that "the difference between the average length of lives of savage and civilized is no true measure of their two lives, considered as aggregate of thoughts, feeling, and action."[1] Not only the length of life, but its fullness determines its definition. Longevity is impossible without successful adaptation to environment. The natural environment is in a constant state of flux and must continuously rebalance itself.

This is equally true of human social environment. The difference between the two—human and non-human nature—is that rationality can aid society's re-balancing; it need not be "red in tooth and claw." A healthy society bespeaks individuals who are altruistic, humane, and just. Sacrifice is no less primordial than self-preservation, though the former is acquired and the latter instinctual. "Except the seed die, itself remains alone."

The martial arts regard all conduct as a type of adaptation to the individual's natural and social environment. One's conduct is "good" or "bad" insofar as it represents a successful or an unsuccessful adaptation.

Thus, like any philosophy, the philosoply of the martial arts is concerned with the good life, particularly the welfare of human life. In man's imperfect state, this includes moral discipline, since both vice and virtue are components in the human make-up.

Happiness, as illustrated in Aristotle's ethics, presents pleasure as good, and its opposite, pain, as bad. But this may be interpreted in too narrow a sense as utilitarian. More fully, happiness is a state of being, not just a passing feeling. It is an activity; since virtuous activity is desirable for its own sake (including pain at times), happiness is a virtuous activity.

While it is normal for a person to live in society, and unusual (possibly abnormal) for him to live alone, it is also healthy to enjoy solitude occasionally. But this solitude must be more than just a vacuous existence. It is certainly not to be equated with solitary confinement. To be healthy, it must involve active contemplation. This means stepping back, as it were, to assess what progress has been made, whether goals should be re-thought, and how the means to achieve goals should be modified.

In practising the martial arts, one learns the *way* of life, not just the skills of living. Ultimately, they demand that one be not merely efficient or expert in skill, but that one master the way.

Students and observers alike are sometimes puzzled by the fact that they must be familiar with methods of concentration, equilibrium, and focus before they can take up the specifics of kicking, breaking, and punching. The truth is, skills (important as they are), are secondary to right motivation. If self-defense were a matter only of protecting oneself against external attack, this might be accomplished with a gun or a dog. While there is nothing wrong with being a sharpshooter, it is limited to marksmanship, and that is all. The martial arts go further. They show a process that must be carried as one carries heart and soul: always and in all things.

To be properly qualified to take up the martial arts, the individual must be purified of self-seeking. He is baptized with the waters of mental cultivation and physical discipline. He must be willing to give up what he has, in order to become what he is to be. Wealth, fame, and social status, possessed for themselves, are only obstacles to the free and powerful spirit of the martial arts.

A candidate for a martial arts school has, by admittance, begun to learn compassion, and how to spend life in the art of total living. Hence, the school is, in a very elevated sense, a sacred place for anyone who respects human dignity and autonomy. That is why students are required to bow at the entrance of the school, bowing toward their potential selves, and pledging their sincerity and loyalty.

Once admitted, the student is shown how to master three powers comprising the weapons of self-defense. These are inner power, outer power, and spiritual power. Inner power refers to health of the body. Outer power refers to the actions one performs and the way one performs them. The repetition of properly executed movements engenders habits of poise, grace, and control that emanate from spiritual power.

Through spiritual power one enters the realms of the unconscious or subconscious, that unique psyche that refines and defines personality. To prevail here is to prevail over all, for it is present in every other power the person exercises. It is manifested in the faultless harmony of a healthy mind in a healthy body. It is at once a prerequisite for, and a result of, the practice of the martial arts. As the martial artist apprehends the needs of each moment, whether on or off the training floor, he simultaneously adopts the proper techniques to meet them. To the observer, such instantaneous precision appears to be reflex or unconscious action. It is, however, actually the result of very deliberate choices, practised to perfection.

A glimpse into the meaning of spiritual power in action can be gained from the following anecdote.

Two monks on pilgrimage came to a river which they must ford. There they saw a girl, dressed in all her finery. She was apparently at a loss as to how to cross the river, as it was high and she did not want her clothes ruined. One of the monks took her on his back, carried her across, and set her on dry ground. As the monks continued on their way, the second monk began to complain.

"Surely," he said, "it is not right to touch a woman; it is against the commandments to have close contact with women. How can you act contrary to the rule for monks?"

The first monk simply walked on in silence for awhile. Then he remarked quietly, "I set her down by the river. But you are still carrying her."

Spiritual power, like a sole light in deepest darkness, is the directive to positive action. Words with essentially religious connotations ("miraculous," "superhuman," "supernatural"), are not uncommon in descriptions of the martial arts in their refined state. Thus, the seemingly impossible is made possible, for in its capacity as a physical exercise as well as a spiritual discipline, the martial arts provide a method of unifying matter and spirit in such a way as infinitely to expand and deepen life.

Those anxious to learn only the outward skills of the martial arts will never master them completely without the more important exercise of spiritual power. They may, in fact, fall into the opposite state of over-confidence. A master gardener, famous for his skill in climbing trees to prune them, tested a student by allowing him to climb a very high tree. Many stood around to watch. The master stood quietly, carefully following every move of his disciple, but never interfering. The student, having pruned the tree, began to descend. When he was only about ten feet from the ground, the master suddenly shouted, "Take care, take care!"

After the young man was safely down, an old man asked the master why he had waited until the student was nearly down before he cautioned him.

"But isn't it obvious?" queried the master. "Right up at the top he was conscious of the danger, and of himself takes care. But near the end where he begins to feel safe, this is when accidents occur." Over-confidence shows a lack of spiritual power.

For all other creatures improvement is largely a matter of chance. Man alone can develop a program that makes of life an art and of himself an artist. The martial arts promote a tranquil happiness and content, unique to each individual. This is the proper entrance to immortality.

The individual outside of this order tries in vain to hold to an impermanent self. The well-rounded person vigorously but calmly tussles with conflicting ideals, bringing himself and them into an alignment that best serves his purposes. He does so under the guidance of a competent master who can provide enlightenment in doubt, and encouragement in times of despair. While the martial artist is never too proud to accept sound advice, he never puts the burden of personal decision on someone else's shoulders. He is simultaneously dependent on and free from others. Two thousand years ago a great teacher, Hillel, said:

> *If I am not for myself,*
> *Then who can be for me?*
> *But if I am only for myself,*
> *Then what am I?*

The answers to both questions are obvious: no one, and nothing, respectively. The art of life goes far beyond mere survival. Physical, psychological, spiritual and sociological elements must develop in close touch with each other, mutually challenging and nourishing the whole person.

An inner voice speaks like a song without words: "Go into the wilderness; you will surely learn something." Venture into the unknown of your potential; you will surely come out the victor.

NOTES TO CHAPTER 5

1. Herbert Spencer, *Principles of Psychology,* Chapter 2.

Chapter 6

THE MARTIAL ARTS AND FREEDOM

Stone walls do not a prison make,
Nor iron bars a cage;
Minds innocent and quiet take
That for an hermitage:
If I have freedom in my love
And in my soul am free,
Angels alone, that soar above,
Enjoy such liberty.
                    —Richard Lovelace

To say that no limited being is free verges on tautology; a person is unfree insofar as he *is* limited. Because human beings are not divine beings, they cannot be absolutely free. A person is limited, for example, by a given physique, more or less developed, subject to pain, disease, and accident. One's mental capacity is conditioned by inheritance and training. Even one's will, prized as the most reserved of possessions, is subject to the influences of passion, suggestion, the unconscious, and ethics.

Therefore, what does "free" mean to a human being? A prisoner is said to have lost his freedom. A person acting with a gun at his head is not free. A ship's captain jettisoning cargo in a storm is surely not acting freely. The psychopath is not free. Starving people cannot be said to be free.

For human beings "free" can never mean totally unshackled. Bertrand Russell observed that complete freedom in an entire life would be possible only for an omnipotent being. "Practicable freedom," he said, "is a matter of degree, dependent on both external circumstances and on the nature of our desires."[1]

"Free" does, however, have meaning, not just as an idea, but in a practical, concrete way. From the point of view of the martial arts, a person is free to make choices in the matters that mean most to him.

> *If I have freedom in my love,*
> *and in my soul am free,*
> *Angels alone, who soar above,*
> *Enjoy such liberty.*

It is quite possible for someone to choose incorrectly or to judge badly; but "freedom" must allow such mistakes. According to Socrates, a rational being does not knowingly choose self-injury or evil.

Freedom means the leisure to dream, to fantasize, to aspire to that which seems good. The individual can pursue his "dream" in reality, if he is free. Innate to such pursuit is the sense of wonder: not just awe, but a genuine curiosity in the "What if...?"

The martial artist does not consider discipleship a loss of freedom. By following a master, one is exercising the freedom to be dominated if that serves one's purposes. In this way, one can bring order out of chaos, certainty out of doubt, wisdom from ignorance.

Some freedoms are built despite risks. The person exercising the right to "create" something finds that it must go in a way he could not anticipate; he lets it take its course. He does not make the experiment fit his preconceived notion of the result, but keeps his mind open to receive something he did not necessarily expect. It is no lack of freedom to have to concede an error, or to have to change one's mind on the basis of evidence or logic.

The martial arts prescribe a program of many rules and much discipline, but that is not contrary to freedom. No one is forced to take up the program against his will. Even then, the program is not exactly the same for any two persons, as each is encouraged—rather, ordered—to individualize the routines to fit each one's personality, needs, and desires.

Transcendental analysis suggests that there are three types of "I" in every person: the parent, the child, and the adult. The free individual can call on any one of these "selves" to make a decision in a specific situation. Although persons adopting *their* way of acting do set up boundaries ("scripts"), they are not less free after adopting them if the choice to do so was free. Furthermore, such persons are constantly re-evaluating, amending, and re-choosing their "life scripts."[2]

The martial artist sees freedom as having the time (leisure) to let his "creations" happen. Most permanent or worthwhile goods do not just

happen out of the blue; they require preparation, gestation, metamorphosis. To every experience, one brings a matrix of life uniquely one's
own. Freedom means the right to be permitted to be unique, sometimes
at the expense of experiencing less, or of experiencing pain. (It is said
that most people use only about one-fifth of their intellectual and
physical potential.)

About 700 years ago a well-known master named Sosya, ripe with
years and honors, lay dying. His students asked him if he was afraid
to die.

"Yes," said the master. "I am afraid to meet my Maker."

"But how can that be?" asked the youths. "You have lived such an
exemplary life. You have led us out of the wilderness of ignorance, like
Moses. Like Solomon, you have judged wisely between us."

Sosya replied, "When I meet my Maker, he will not ask, 'Have you
been Moses or Solomon?' He will ask, 'Have you been Sosya?' "

So, freedom has its burden. It is easier to follow wise counsel than
to give it wisely. What is more, freedom does not come freely. It is said
that, for freedom to disappear from the face of the earth it is sufficient
that free persons do nothing about it. While it is undesirable to set
unrealistic goals for oneself, it is equally undesirable to under-rate one's
talents. If one cannot scale Mount Everest, it is no dishonor to climb
Mont Blanc; if one cannot save a thousand persons, it is still good to
save one.

What this all boils down to for the martial artist is to be allowed to
choose an identity and to be permitted to live it out. The idea is well expressed by William James in a letter to his wife.

> A man's character is discernible in the mental or moral attitude
> in which, when it came upon him, he felt himself most deeply
> and intensely active and alive. At such moments there is a voice
> inside which speaks up and says, 'This is the real me!'...
>
> (Such an experience always includes)...an element of active ten-
> sion, of holding my own, as it were, and trusting outward
> things to perform their part so as to make it a full harmony,
> but without any guaranty that they will. Make it a guaranty...
> and the attitude immediately becomes to my consciousness stag-
> nant and stingles. Take away the guaranty, and I feel (provided
> I am überhaupt), a sort of deep enthusiastic bliss, of bitter
> willingness to do and suffer anything...and which, although it

is a mere mood or emotion to which I can give no form in
words, authenticates itself to me as the deepest principle of all
active and theoretic determination which I possess.[3]

This is markedly subjective, and would be incomplete without its objective complement. One's chosen identity must also be recognized and confirmed by others. Short of that, both freedom and identity are illusions.

The martial arts do not tell a person what identity he *ought* to strive for. To set up a hypothetical "if you were such and so..." in place of "because you are such and so..." would be ludicrous and futile. An individual must be allowed his conscious desires, reflecting his personal idosyncracies and temperament. The variety of identities is as multitudinous as there are (several billions!) people on earth. What the martial arts do is to set the goals as high as possible, so that after every milestone is reached, the person knows there is another further on.

Since there is no *one* earthly good (or sum of goods) that everyone must desire, the martial arts emphasize that, once an identity or goal has been responsibly chosen, the individual may confidently work towards it. A warrior in battle must fight, not contemplate the meaning of war.

At the beginning of this chapter it was said that an individual possesses freedom to the extent that circumstances permit him to realize his desires and the goal he aims to reach. Thus, individuals are generally regarded as unfree to the extent that they act, not as they wish for the good as they see it, but as they or others think they *ought* to act. The martial arts readily admit that goals and desires can and do conflict with set rules. But exactly what is right and what is wrong has always been contentious. Kant, for example, claimed that an action was right if, and only if, one acted with respect to the moral law; this, however, does not solve the problem of conflicting duties when one must tell a lie to save a friend. Utilitarians were no more successful in inventing a cover-all principle; for how could anyone predict the total consequences of an action which are at the same time the criteria of the action?

In practice, of course, "right" (for freedom to act according to one's conscience) is not always upheld against "might." It is now widely accepted, for instance, that the ideals of the American colonists in seceding from England were right, but that those of the South trying to secede from the Union were wrong. History calls one a rebellion against oppression, the other a revolution against a rightly elected government. One might conclude, that to set up rules one cannot enforce, is an exercise in futility. Not so. Force may rule temporarily, but there will always be those who cherish freedom passionately enough to make it prevail in the end.

A case in point can again be drawn from history, this time from the Greeks in the era of Spartan and Athenian ascendancy.

The Spartans, aggressive and warlike, were making their influence felt among their neighbors around the eighth century B.C. They, unlike the Homeric Greeks, had no interests other than physical excellence. They were determined to produce strong people, subservient to the state: healthy men who became crack soldiers, healthy women to rear robust children. They had no time for science, philosophy, art or literature. For a time they managed to rise to military and political supremacy, but not for long. Their suppression of freedom, their unwillingness to develop and exchange ideas were major factors in their downfall. They seemed superior in the martial arts, but that is impossible unless one achieves the excellence of the whole person. One must be free to suggest initiatives even in the strategies of war.

The Athenians, on the other hand, springing from a culture similar to that of the Spartans, took another way. They developed in a more characteristically democratic, progressive, intellectual society. They went to war when attacked, but they did not make a fetish of the military. Their education stressed mind and spirit more than physique. Their interests in beauty, harmony, art, and architecture are legacies that remain to this day. From them nations have inherited Olympic competitions as well as the best in art and thought.

However, they went to the other extreme of cultivating the mind while neglecting the body; they spouted theories, forgetting the man of action. Physical fitness fell into decline as luxurious living came into vogue. Instead of being themselves athletes, they were content to observe the performance of others. So they, too, lost the supremacy.

From the point of view of the martial arts, each of these civilizations neglected the major principle that the whole person must be free to develop. The Spartans sacrificed individual freedom for the collective strength of the state; the Athenians directed individual freedom only to the mind; and so each lost an essential dimension in human progress. Robots cannot compete with intelligence; but wisdom untranslated into action dies.

So the martial artist is detached, yes, but not from commitment; he is not uncaring. He is passionate, yes, but with decorum; he constructs and orders. He takes risks, yes, but not in folly; only as full living presents these. Yet there is one more point to be made.

When all is said and done, the martial artist still leaves room for inspiration, for the intuitive, for the prodigy, for the quantum leap. There will always be another world to discover when freedom has won the last one.

NOTES TO CHAPTER 6

1. Bertrand Russell, "Freedom and Government," *Freedom: Its Meaning,* ed. R.N. Anshen (Harcourt-Brace, New York: 1940), p. 251.
2. Claude Steiner, *Scripts People Live By* (Random House, New York: 1974).
3. William James, *The Letters of William James,* ed. Henry James, Vol. I (The Atlantic Monthly Press, Boston: 1920), p. 79.

Chapter 7

THE MARTIAL ARTS AND DISCIPLINE

The artist descends within himself,
*   and in that lonely region of stress and strife,*
if he be deserving and fortunate,
*   he finds the terms of his appeal.*
His appeal is made to our less obvious capacities:
*   to that part of our nature which,*
because of the warlike conditions of existence,
*   is necessarily kept out of sight.*
The artist appeals to that part of our being
*   which is not dependent on wisdom:*
to that in us which is a gift and not an acquisition.
*   He speaks to our capacity for delight and wonder,*
to the sense of mystery surrounding our lives;
*   to our sense of pity, and beauty, and pain;*
to the latent feeling of fellowship with all creation.
*   —Joseph Conrad*

A once popular method of instilling discipline and self-control in the young was expressed in the adage: spare the rod and spoil the child. Today the pendulum has swung to the other extreme of unguided permissiveness. The discipline of the martial arts lies between unreasonable restraint and total license.

Persons capable of assimilating knowledge are of two kinds traditionally associated with the scientific and the mystic. These are investigative and intuitive, respectively. In general, Western thought favors the rational and investigative approach, while the East follows the more mystical line of thought. The martial arts emphasize the complementary nature of both intuition and logic; in their idea of discipline, however, they place a greater emphasis on the Oriental preference for intuition and inspiration than on a strictly Western interpretation of the term.

The martial artist is neither only a scholar nor an expert in physical routines. Rather he is a person wise enough to know that learning, like art, has one chief purpose: to show man his own face. When a child first senses the use of his own mind, he ecstatically revels in the power of his intellect. The free use of his mind at this stage increases his development by leaps and bounds. If, however, only his intellect grows, while he remains physically and emotionally immature, he is no better off—in fact, may be much worse off—than the unlettered ploughman who is, at least, leading a balanced life.

The twentieth century has produced more than its share of this clever schoolboy type of intellectual. The West is too "clever" in the poorer sense of the word. The highest praise was bestowed on Shakespeare's Brutus when his eulogist declared, "This was a man!" Such a person has not grown, as a weed, rank, but with slow, steady discipline.

In civilization the correct mixture of intellect, feeling, and will has always been, and continues to be, a controversial matter. William James's pragmatism becomes a revolt against intellectualism or the over-use of logic in inquiry. Turning away from rationale to fact, away from abstractions to concrete experience, the practical person turns "toward action and towards power." James's revolt against intellectualism emphasizes experience without interpretation, thus rendering experience barren and meaningless.

The ideal human—though unattainable in full—is the ultimate goal of the martial artist. Such a person is what Confucius calls "the son of the lord." In its wider connotations, "Chun-tzu" is "any person of good breeding." Confucius' Chun-tzu always acts according to the rules of propriety which have become so much a part of his nature that he can never violate them. His uprightness, the expression of his nature, blends perfectly with that proper amount of refinement so that he is neither pedantic nor crude. With a firm will and an appearance that is always calm, his humanity keeps him from unwarranted anxiety, his wisdom guards against perplexity, and his courage dispels debilitating fears. "He first practises what he preaches," say Confucius, "and then he preaches what he practises."[1]

Above all, the disciplined person seeks and treasures the essence of things, for his mind is capable of sifting the wheat from the chaff. Such a person stands in stark contrast to the inevitably dependent product of a technologically-oriented civilization. This becomes clearer as one contrasts Western thought with the Oriental way of thinking and living as described in *The Great Learning,* the Confucian work which teaches great virtue, the love of others, and the pursuit of the highest good. In order that great virtue might prevail, one must first cultivate oneself to perfection, put one's own house in order, then bring the same harmonious order to the state, and finally extend it to embrace all mankind.

In this the martial artist is like Nietzsche's Zarathustra, wishing to be the creator of value, giving personal meaning to such terms as *good* and *evil.* Like Confucius' Chuntzu, he is concerned with the substance and not the outer trappings. He looks to secure a perfect balance in the faculties of intellect, emotion, and will so that his wisdom reveals itself in every detail of his action.

While granting emotion and desire their place, the martial artist is not dominated by them; he is able to distinguish between what is to be feared and what is to be loved. This ability is so matched with his courage as to eliminate even fear of death. He is not unduly worried about God, or what is to come after death, for his resolute acceptance of death leads him confidently to immortality, just as his rectification of mind makes it possible for him to complete the "investigation of things." His perpetual request is:

> *From the unreal lead me to the real!*
> *From darkness lead me to light!*
> *From death lead me to immortality!*[2]

The discipline of knowledge in the Oriental view is to be used toward attaining moral excellence. *The Great Learning* does not urge the individual to continue in the accumulation of objective facts which, as the martial arts admit, are endless and often confusing. The boxing champion, for example, may be admired even though he is morally corrupt. The head of organized crime is admired and feared by some for his energy and bravery. Even among martial artists there may be those who desire recognition through mastery of certain skills rather than a totally upright character, but they will never be genuine martial artists.

The Great Learning marks the differences between the essence and the outward features of things. The essence of the martial arts is its spirit, the outward features are the many techniques it teaches.

> *The master was asked by a monk: 'I have been with you for*
> *three years, and received no teaching from you. Why?'*

The master replied, 'Have I not been teaching you ever since you arrived?'
'When did you give me any teaching?' asked the monk.
The master said, 'When you brought me tea, I received it from you. When you bowed to me, I inclined my head to you. When did I not teach you?'
While the monk was still pondering this, the master added:
'When you look, just look. If you worry about it, you won't get the point.'
On this, the monk awakened. [3]

Usually the master's knowledge is not contained in a clearly specified set of boundaries; thus, to those who do not know what to learn from him, the master appears to be nothing more than an ordinary man. It is in this sense that the master's warning, "When you look, just look," is to be understood. That is, when one looks one must do so not merely with the eyes, but also with the mind. This entails vision, not just sight.

⌐The intuitive approach to knowledge and discipline can be directly applied to the martial arts. The student approaches learning as though he were coming to a forest. Although he may get lost and go astray, when he finally emerges he is able to tell both what a tree is and what the forest is. This is the intuitive method. Another student might be satisfied with knowing the tree, then rationalizing that the forest must be only a tree repeated many times. Such a student likewise too often understands the martial arts only as a certain combination of punching and kicking techniques. This exemplifies the investigative and analytical method of learning. ⌐

On the whole, the Oriental mind is not as predisposed to pondering the supernatural or the afterlife as is the Western. In this respect, Confucius' silence on the supernatural is eloquent. In *The Analects* he neither defends nor attempts to destroy the prevailing ideas about the world of the spirits. Indeed, he instructed his disciples to keep their minds on the affairs of men and not be bothered by analyses of the spirits, as they must first learn enough about this life before inquiring into the next. This world provided ample material for full-time life study; one could deal with the hereafter when one got to it. Sincerity in ritual required, of course, the admission of spirits; therefore, one had to conduct the sacrificial rites to one's ancestors "as if they were present" and to the spirits also "as if they were present." Beyond this, he said, one should not go. It was enough "to respect the spirits and stay away from them."

If one understands that the discipline of the martial arts is a matter of rectifying or emptying the mind of dross, and that by so emptying it, one can even accept death unflinchingly, then one can also understand how in the Orient one can meaningfully discuss immortality without introducing the notion of a punitive or rewarding god. Taosim illustrates this well. The pacifism of Taoism is not that of the humanitarian but of the old rogue, based not on universal love but on a convincing type of subtle wisdom.

> *What is in the end to be shrunk*
> *Must first be stretched.*
> *Whatever is to be weakened*
> *Must begin by being made strong.*
> *What is to be overthrown*
> *Must begin by being set up.*
> *He who would be a taker*
> *Must begin as a giver.*
> *This is called 'dimming' one's light.*
> *It is thus that the soft overcomes the hard*
> *And the weak the strong.*
> *It is best to leave the fish down in his pool;*
> *Best to leave the State's sharpest weapons*
> *where none can see them.*[4]

There is not a more effectively preached sermon on the strength of weakness, the victory of the peace-maker, and the advantage of lying low to gain one's end.

Taoist principles were attributed to a past golden age in order to make their philosophical innovation seem conservative and therefore more palatable to the people of the time. During this golden age, it was said, people lived naturally, wearing clothes they had woven and eating foods they had grown, and all creatures of the earth and the sky lived together in harmony. People practised virtue unself-consciously and did not argue over the logical niceties of the casuist. Thus, all things acted naturally, without knowledge, having no "axe to grind," without un-natural desires, and without artificial restraints. All things existed in harmony because all were able to express their natures spontaneously. However, the arrival of culture heroes brought a disruption of values to this community which gradually lost its golden age. People submitted to the shackles of convention, and the world became confused because the Tao was obscured. The Taoists had resisted the way of a society that they saw as an agent of the corruption of man, separating him from his true nature.

The practical consequence of man's corruption by society and by errors arising from his senses is that people deliberately exert themselves for unnatural ends. Embroiled in politics and loud arguments, they fight with one another and feel frustrated in their search for fame. They arouse envy and constantly live in fear of death. They rush into risks to save seconds, only to squander time by the hour later on.

> *An elder monk on his pilgrimage one evening put up in a temple where he talked with another monk also on pilgrimage. The two found that they had much in common, and decided next morning to continue together. When they came to a river, the ferry boat had just left. The elder sat down to await its return. His new friend continued, walking over the water. Halfway across he turned and motioned to the other, calling, 'You can do it, too. Just have confidence and step on.' But the elder shook his head and remained seated. 'If you are frightened,' rejoined the other, 'I'll help you across. You see I can do it.' Again the elder shook his head. The other walked across, and there waited until the ferry had brought his friend over. 'Why did you lag behind like that?' he asked. 'And what have you gained by hurrying like that?' replied the other. 'Had I known what you were like, I would not have taken up company with you.' And wishing him goodbye, the elder continued alone.* [5]

Lao-tzu's admonition is:

> *The best charioteers do not rush ahead;*
> *The best fighters do not make displays of wrath.*
> *The greatest conqueror wins without joining issue;*
> *The best user of men acts as though he were their inferior.*
> *That is called the power that comes of not contending.*
> *Is called the capacity to use men,*
> *The secret of being mated to heaven, to what is of old...*
>
> *The Wise Man chooses to be last*
> *And so becomes the first of all.* [6]

Once, in a whimsical mood, a person categorized people into three groups: pessimists, optimists, and fatalists. The pessimist, he said, believes that if anything can go wrong, it will; the fatalist believes that he has no control over his life, so he sits back and waits for things to happen to him; the optimist believes he can and must be in charge of his life, and takes positive steps to achieve this. He not only reaches his goals but has the rewarding sense of accomplishment as he constructs his world.

The martial artist identifies with the optimist, of course. He knows that he gains nothing by undue hurry. Though he may travel alone, he is not lonesome because he is with nature. He envies no one, and is envied by none. He is free from fear, free from anxiety, and free from failure because his mind is right. His attitude, like a stream of water, is steady; his action, like the rolling waves, is ever forward. Success is perpetually within his grasp.

A positive mental attitude is essential to successful discipline in the martial arts. With determination and confidence the martial artist continues even when he knows that his efforts may not bring immediate results. His depth of conviction buoy him up in time of trial, as it did Atticus Finch in Harper Lee's *To Kill A Mockingbird*. This small-town Southern lawyer chooses to defend a Black unjustly accused of raping a white woman. That Atticus will lose the case is a foregone conclusion because popular opinion is strongly against him and he must face an all-white jury. His children question his wisdom in acting as he does. Atticus explains:

> Sometimes we have to make the best of things, and the way we conduct ourselves when the chips are down—well, all I can say is, when you and Jem are grown, maybe you'll look back on this with some compassion and some feeling that I didn't let you down. This case is something that goes to the essence of man's conscience—I couldn't go to church and worship God if I didn't try to help that man. Before I can live with other folks I've got to live with myself. The one thing that doesn't abide by majority rule is a person's conscience.[7]

When the martial artist meets a set-back, he does not sit and brood about it. Chalking it up to experience, he tries to learn something from his mistakes. He knows that results may not come easily and he is willing to endure the rough times because of the faith he has in himself.

This confidence, however, does not result from either argument or analysis. Rather, it arises from a healthy synthesis of intuition and reason. The martial artist strives for a return to the proven standard which recognizes that cleverness belongs to the intellect alone, while wisdom is a complex of intellect, emotion, spirit and body.

NOTES TO CHAPTER 7

1. *The Analects* in *The Human Way in Ancient China: Essential Works of Confucianism,* ed. and trans. by Ch'u Chai and Winberg Chai (Bantam Books, New York: 1965), p. 31.
2. Swami Nikhilananda, *The Upanishads,* Abridged Edition (Harper & Row, New York, 1964), p. 189.
3. *The Wisdom of the Zen Masters*, edited by I. Schloegl (Sheldon Press, London, 1976), p. 75.
4. *Lao Tzu, Tao Te Ching,* ed. R. B. Blakney (Mentor Books, New York, 1955), p. 89.
5. *The Wisdom of the Zen Masters,* edited by I. Schloegl, pp. 42-43
6. Lao-tzu, *Tao Te Ching*, 7, ed. by R.B. Blakney (New York: 1955), p. 38.
7. Harper Lee, *To Kill A Mockingbird*. (J.B. Lippincott, New York: 1960), p. 109.

Chapter 8

THE MARTIAL ARTS AND TRANSCENDENCE

As to me I know of nothing else but miracles,
Whether I walk the streets of Manhattan...
Or wade with naked feet along the beach...
Or stand under the trees in the woods,
Or talk by day with any one I love...
Or watch honey-bees busy around the hive...
Or animals feeding in the fields...
Or the wonderfulness of the sundown...
Or the exquisite delicate thin curve of the new moon...
These with the rest, one and all, are to me miracles.
                          —Walt Whitman

One can grow and develop in the martial arts only if one follows the basic principles, be one's heritage Oriental or Western. Recent years have, unfortunately often witnessed dramatic changes for the worse in the practice of the martial arts in the western world. The genuine spirit of the arts seems to have faded; people reveal but a shallow interest in them because they lack an understanding of their purpose and practice. Exploitation of the martial arts to serve economic and political gain is a travesty of the martial arts.

Since the origin of the arts is religious rather than secular, the practitioner seeks improvement, even as did the monks who did so in the hope of earning a glorious afterlife. The prime object is never victory over opponents, but victory over self. The true practitioner seeks transcendence.

> *It is wisdom to know others;*
> *It is enlightenment to know one's self.*
>
> *The conqueror of men is powerful;*
> *the master of himself is strong.* [1]

Because people frequently classify other persons as stereotypes rather than individuals, they have separated all mankind into East and West.

On the one hand, there is the "Eastern" way of life: alien, quaint, mysterious. On the other hand is the "Western" lifestyle: humane, normal, rational. Orientals, it is claimed, give priority to spiritual realization, to a productive life of personal fulfillment. Westerners, by contrast, primarily seek material satisfaction and pleasure, living a life of consumption rather than conservation. In this light, Orientals are contemplative, spiritual, and stoic; Westerners are practical, materialistic, and hedonistic.

These notions are, of course, gross generalizations, very much to be guarded against. A martial artist transcends such over-simplifications. Kipling's "East is East, and West is West, and ne'er the twain shall meet" is simply no longer true. Kipling had no way of knowing the extent of today's cultural diffusion whereby both East and West have borrowed materials, ideas, and mores from each other, adapting them to their particular needs.

Some people claim they understand Oriental culture though they are ignorant of the essential differences between East and West. They will, for instance, pronounce "professionally" on Oriental cuisine as if they were experts in the field, having tasted only chop suey (which is no Oriental dish at all!). Likewise, they understand Karate as a kind of boxing, and Judo as a form of wrestling. For them the martial arts are a conglomeration of deadly "chops." This is, of course, utter rubbish. The preceding pages of this book should effectively have laid that ghost by now. The reader would know that the martial artist is one who affirms life, is involved, heart and soul, in the process of total living.

This life is a happy one, and is characterized by certain recognizable qualities. The first of these is coherence. Ends and means are clearly sorted and arranged in a harmonious perspective of priorities. This ordering of goals is based on the martial artist's judgment of the comparative importance of goals open to him. When the individual is faced with making a choice, the lesser gives way to the greater, the transient to the permanent. In this manner, his life-plan is integrated into a unified whole.

Another quality marking a happy life is that the chosen way expresses the individual's self concept. The ordering of the plan results from the individual's own decisions, made in light of personal value options. Not only is life integrated, making possible the pursuit of long-range as well as short-range goals, but it is also self-directed. A person's happiness in this respect depends on his being in control. This does not mean rigidity. It does mean a creative growth within chosen guidelines, that goes on as long as life itself.

Such a life, as has already been pointed out, requires education and discipline. The training procedure in the martial arts might be compared to an investment in real estate or jewelry, the value of which increases as it matures. In contradistinction to this, buying clothes, automobiles, or other items that lose value as they are used up, are no "investment" for long-range rewards. If the martial arts practitioner concentrates on (or "invests in") one basic technique a day, striving for complete perfection, he will, after even one year, have accumulated a wealth of techniques that no money can buy and no thief can steal. The individual does not *have* these qualities so much as he *is* them.

The martial arts, even as self-defense, are an investment in life as they are always concerned with the total self. Self is not merely a physical entity, but involves both body and spirit. To the "spirit" is ascribed not only moral responsibility but the decision-making apparatus of the human. It is this point that differentiates the martial arts from western sport where one seems to defend only one's physical self and where one's fundamental morality or spiritual self is not the principal focus; winning is.

"Self is a crucial concept in the martial arts. It requires that the self be clearly defined, defended, and eventually transcended. An individual's ability within certain limits to remake himself and determine what kind of self he will become is what chiefly distinguishes human from sub-human existence.

Self has no tangibly fixed limits as do things which are inanimate or dead. To distinguish one country from another there are boundaries. Likewise, Tom's body is clearly marked from Dick's. However, when Tom and Dick are conversing, it is not so easy to "locate" their ideas as they come out in the conversation. As soon as one passes beyond purely conventional and technical conceptions of self, one is forced to acknowledge that the self is not a determinate unit like a physical body. One can never say, "Precisely *this* constitutes the personality of an individual." Personhood, in other words, is self-transcendent.

An obvious way in which self can be seen to transcend itself is in its possession of knowledge. The phenomenon that each of us is likely to know most intimately is our own body. But is this body an object which the self knows or is it a part of the self? The answer, of course, varies, depending on one's interpretation or emphasis at the moment. Furthermore, some parts of the body seem more intimately a part of the self than others.

The self also transcends assignable boundaries through partial identification with other selves. William James says, "a man has as many social selves as there are individuals who recognize him and carry an image of him in their minds. To wound any one of these images is to wound him." In the martial arts the relation of self to self appears to be a form of loyalty which may be called "efforts at finding the self in others." Such loyalty is the basis of all genuine friendship.

The self is also self-conscious; that is, reflective. The inscription over the grotto of the Delphic Oracle read: "Know thyself." It is still one of the most profound of moral teachings. It is what Wordsworth called "the prime and heaven-sprung adage of the olden time." For to know oneself is the first step toward taking responsible charge of oneself. It bids one know and govern the kingdom which is rightfully one's own. Only as master of self can the individual successfully perform his role in society.

One may also transcend self through mysticism, through which the individual soul conquers its individuality by becoming one with God. The central truth of Hindiusm, for example, is epitomized in its constantly repeated phrase, "Atman is Brahman." The real nature and destiny of the individual as distinguished from his surface personality, is identical to the infinite cosmic self or Brahman. A homelier but no less expressive similitude is given by the Chinese Tao philosopher, Chuang-tze. It must be quoted in its full length.

> Prince Hui's cook was cutting up a bullock. Every blow of
> his hand, every heave of his shoulders, every tread of his foot,
> every thrust of his knee, every whshh of rent flesh, every chhk
> of the chopper, was in perfect harmony—rhythmical like a
> dance of the Mulberry Grove, simultaneous like the chords of
> the Ching Sou.

'Well done!' cried the Prince, 'Yours is skill indeed.'

'Sire,' replied the cook, 'I have always devoted myself to Tao. It is better than skill. When I first began to cut up bullocks, I saw before me simply whole bullocks. After three years' practice, I saw no more whole animals. And now I work with my mind and not with my eye. When my senses bid me stop but my mind urges me on, I fall back upon eternal principles. I follow such openings or cavities as there may be according to the natural constitution of the animal. I do not attempt to cut through joints, still less through large bones.

'A good cook changes his chopper once a year—because he cuts. An ordinary cook, once a month—because he hacks. But I have had this chopper nineteen years, and although I have cut up many thousand bullocks, its edge is as if fresh from the whetstone. For at the joints there are always interstices, and the edge of a chopper being without thickness, it remains only to insert that which is without thickness into such an interstice. By these means the interstice will be enlarged, and the blade will find plenty of room. It is thus that I have kept my chopper for nineteen years as though fresh from the whetstone.

'Nevertheless, when I come upon a hard part where the blade meets with a difficulty, I am all caution. I fix my eye on it. I stay my hand, and gently apply my blade, until with a hwah *the part yields like earth crumbling to ground. Then I take out my chopper, and stand up, and look around, and pause, until with an air of triumph I wipe my chopper and put it carefully away.'*

'Bravo!' cried the Prince. 'From the words of this cook I have learned how to take care of my life.'[2]

It is difficult to put such a philosophical idea into words. One cannot really express the inner experience and achievement of the cook in words. But one thing in Chaun-tze's teaching is clear: one must be patient and make an investment in order to master any field. In the martial arts this is especially important to those who, after a certain level, would rather practise free-fighting than stay with the routines. In such circumstances the cook's advice might well be, "So, if you have spent almost all your time indulging in free-fighting instead of investing it in basics, how many sophisticated techniques and advanced movements can you truly be prepared to perform?"

This theme of self-commitment and dedication recurs again and again in the martial arts. They are religious in the sense that their goals are compatible with and complementary to most religions, whether Oriental or Western. The mastery of the martial arts, for example, goes hand in hand with the development of character. Some specialists claim that discipline is religious insofar as it affects habits of right and wrong, and provides the deepest motivation for human action.

Paradoxically, hedonists seeking pleasure as a conscious goal in life are often those who gain very little pleasure from life. If those who generally abuse their minds and bodies for temporal gratification would invest their time and effort in sound training as in the martial arts, they could not only enjoy their daily lives more, but would also probably live a longer and healthier life.

Self-transcendence is closely related to man's gift of imagination. Although some degree of imagination, of being able to visualize alternative possibilities of thought and action, is common to most humans, individuals differ in their levels of imaginative power. Consequently, they differ in their potential for moral goodness and perfection. The martial artist accepts as a self-evident truth man's ability to identify himself with far-away objects, with other people, and with attainable ideals. This is accomplished through imagination.

One might reasonably conclude, then, that the martial arts are more akin to religious thought than to sport. This closeness becomes even more evident when one recalls that most of the martial arts originated with monks. To those who know what the martial arts are, such recent phenomena as contact karate or boxing versus wrestling for immediate economic and political ends are grotesque caricatures of the genuine art. Basic principles differentiate the martial arts from western sport. This may be difficult for those unfamiliar with Oriental culture to understand. Transcending self is not accomplished by the use of a bag of magic tricks. Perpetual rebirth comes with each new improvement of the old self. The common denominator to all is the individual who accomplishes these feats. The practice of the martial arts gives buoyancy and balance to these unceasing efforts.

NOTES TO CHAPTER 8

1. Lao-tze, *Tao Te Ching,* ed. R.B. Blakney, New York: 1955), p. 86.
2. Lao-tze, quoted by Chuang tzu, *Chuang tzu, Mystic, Moralist, and Social Reformer.* Translated from Chinese by Herbert A. Giles. (Shanghai: 1926) Chapter 3.

Chapter 9

THE MARTIAL ARTS IN ACTION

*Lord, give me the serenity to accept the
things I cannot change, the courage to
change the things I can, and the wisdom
to know the difference.*
                              —*Old Irish Saying*

In mythology Prometheus stole fire from Mount Olympus and gave it to mankind. For this he was cruelly punished by Zeus because fire was to be a property of the gods alone. Anyone having it was a threat to the gods themselves.

Today this myth is interpreted to mean that the faculty of rationality (the fire of inspiration) is that god-like element which raises man above all other animals. If, however, the fire is untended, it flickers and dies. Therefore, in the martial arts, theory must be translated to action if it is to live.

Through conscious and deliberate repetition of the same action, nerve paths are established, until these actions are so deeply engrained that they become spontaneous, virtually reflex. Repetition of the same form or technique does not become boring because the student performs each repetition as though it were the first—with an inquiring mind—determined that each performance will be a newly improved one, uniquely his. Once he has met the standards set by his own conscience, in accord with his potential, he need fear no one's judgment of him. In no way presumptuous, he is simply secure in act. He is gentle with the surly, loyal to his friends, and fierce in opposition to oppression, either of himself or of others.

To strike a happy balance, one must understand well the doctrine of the mean in the context of searching for perfection in virtue through the martial arts. The moral as well as the technical principles of the martial arts are in agreement with the idea that the highest good lies between two extremes. Moderation is the hallmark of culture. Confucius'

Chun-tzu avoids the extreme.

Westerners have no difficulty in accepting this concept of virtue. Furthermore, the good is seen to be that for which all strive. For man this is, of course, happiness, the full realization of his potential. Since man is a rational creature, the good for him is the activity of the soul, in accordance with reason, revealed in action.

> Now virtue is concerned with emotions and actions; in excess or
> deficiency, these miss the mark, whereas the median is praised
> and constitutes success. But both praise and success are signs of
> virtue or excellence. Consequently, virtue is a mean in that it
> aims at the median. [1]

Confucius calls this "jen" or humanity. It is the perfect virtue of human beings, the only road to the peace and harmony of society. He who embraces the principle of *jen* will treat others gently and humanely, and for him everything will go well. The mean between two extremes of conduct is practised only by the superior person, the true gentleman.

> It waits for the proper man and then it is trodden. Hence, it is
> said, 'Only by perfect virtue can the perfect path in all its
> courses be realized.' Therefore, the superior man honors his vir-
> tuous nature and maintains constant inquiry and study, seeking
> to carry it out to its breadth and greatness, so as to omit none of
> the most exquisite and minute points which it embraces, and to
> raise it to its greatest height and brilliancy, so as to pursue the
> course of the mean. [2]

This is essentially the same as the Aristotelian standard of a great-souled man. He is

> primarily concerned with honor and dishonor. From great
> honors and those that good men confer upon him he will derive
> a moderate amount of pleasure, convinced that he is only getting
> proper due, or even less...He will, of course, also have a
> moderate attitude toward wealth, power, and every manner of
> good or bad luck that may befall him...He will show his stature
> in his relations with men of eminence and fortune, but will be
> unassuming toward those of moderate means. [3]

In the practice of the martial arts, this spells out acting with wisdom, humanity, and fortitude. The martial artist acts justly, exerting an exact amount of firmness and leniency. He is prudent, judging the right application of force and gentleness, finding a nice balance between indulgence and austerity.

It must be made clear that the mean spoken of here is not arithmetic; it is not mechanically calculated. The proper amount of food, say, for a wrestler would undoubtedly be too much for the office-bound businessman. Since it is impossible to have fixed standards that will serve as mean for all in every circumstance, one must use the mean only as a guide, making adjustments to more or less as required by time, place, and the individual.

In the end, the perfect martial artist is a very rare specimen indeed, if only because few persons ever have the need to demonstrate the exercise of all virtue in an outstanding way. However, the martial artist will become skilled in inspiring others to imitation, not in slavish conformity, but through creative imagination. He will evince genuine and proper respect both for himself and for others in the knowledge that each individual has an inherently unique worth. His discipline will be self-discipline. His mean lies in the balance between egoism and altruism.

In the martial arts, the term "self-defense" means a benefit to all, since an important part of oneself must come from others. It is as vital to preserve and defend what is good in one's friends and foes as it is to maintain one's own welfare. The natural condition of mankind is to struggle with the odds; by correctly implementing one's powers, the result is a harmonious, creative life.

From yet another point of view, the active martial arts practitioner is seeking Nirvana, the final goal of all previous "incarnations." Traveling the path toward Nirvana, however, is not an act of self-extinction. Rather, it is an act of wise self-interest which comes from the realization of the true character of the human soul and its intrinsic unity with the World Spirit. The ordinances of Manu state:

> Learn the Kharma which is followed by the learned and good, by those ever free from spite and passions, and which is acknowledged by the mind.
>
> Selfishness is not praiseworthy, yet unselfishness exists not here; for the study of the Vedas is for selfish ends, and the practice of rites according to the Vedas...
>
> Yet, one rightly occupied in those acts goes to the world of the immortals, and gets all his desires here as hoped for.[4]

This combination of self-realization and other-worldliness is the reason that Indian teaching, though metaphysical and devotional in nature, is, nevertheless, not sacrificial. It demands the joyful fulfillment of one's specific destiny, duty, and mission: one's Dharma. This fulfillment can be achieved only through maturity gained in the various phases of development. Maturity, however, pre-supposes a healthy understanding of the meaning of survival and self-preservation, that it is neither complete self-interest nor extreme self-sacrifice. The martial arts declare a reasoned self-preservation as the mean between these two extremes.

Virtue does not consist in self-abnegation or in mere negative control of passions, but in self-expansion and the attainment of good. The good person is the strong person. Repentance and humility as signs of weakness have only a slight value, and pity, so far as it is empty feeling, must be discouraged. This self-assertion, however, is not anti-social, since people are most useful to people. Usefulness is practicable only insofar as one is a positive force and has something of one's own to give. To be anything for another, one must first be something to oneself.

While most persons desire the presence of other persons, his normal fears and desires will make this sometimes distressing and dangerous. In order to satisfy desires and calm fears, one must find the way best suited to live with others. In this context, while egoism is based on self-interest without regard for others, altruism prescribes the finding of one's highest welfare in the welfare of others. The object is to find the positive elements of each in a single expression.

The egoist looks after himself and no one else, perhaps at the expense of others. But egoism has both a positive and a negative side. Egoism, for example, leads one to desire wide recognition, and seeks both mental and physical reward for work done; this could lead to selfishness, and so far would be negative. But through goal-orientation, egoism also builds self-confidence, and urges one to protect physical and mental well-being.

The martial arts do not deny that man is motivated by desire, and that desires are chiefly egocentric. Even an apparent altruism can have selfish motives. One might help another because it makes one feel superior. Every person has the right to use his skills for his own sake. But the martial arts also maintain that a harmonious society is possible if individuals in it can use a balance of desire and fear, to create a situation in which each person can be fairly secure with the other.

In action, the martial artist does not feel threatened by his sharing of knowledge and strength. In fact, exclusiveness has a detrimental effect on stability and the capacity to make informed decisions. Flexibility in adjusting to others' needs, however, must not be construed as wishy-washiness. Nor is constancy to be confused with stubborness. Knowing one's strengths and weaknesses, one can work out the mean between these two extremes.

The martial arts, while continuously up-dating action to changing times, still look to their roots in Oriental beginnings. They remain true to the spirit of the traditions handed down through the centuries. The best features of the ancient warriors, the flower of youth, still blossoms today. One still finds the epitome of true courage and loyalty, as among the hwarang-do of old. Like the Japanese samurai, today's martial artists are still known for their honesty and compassion, their mystical interpretation of power and aesthetic sensitivity. The religious influence of monasteries is still evident in the acceptance of responsibility to duty in protecting private and communal interests. They seek the refinement of morals by avoiding degenerative or merely frivolous amusements. They cultivate a sense of truth and beauty by reading and writing poetry, by composing music and playing musical instruments. They prefer games that require intelligence rather than chance. They resort to the outdoors, living close to nature, testing their ability to endure hardship and solitude. By the exercise of contemplation they learn to think through problems, developing a philosophy of long-range goals and enlightened values. They become serviceable as able leaders and dependable followers.

The medieval Western world exemplified a comparable ethic in the order of knighthood. In its ideal form, members practised personal integrity, and dedicated their services to the poor, the helpless, and the oppressed.

In retrospect, one must ask what it was that gave the enduring quality of practical action to a military art which had its beginnings in such ancient times, yet persists in a very real way even to our own day. The quality is elusive because it is both collective and individual. One must refer to mystic and universal elements that have been and will continue to be applied in every age because they are integral to human excellence. No one quality is the answer, but an essential ingredient is that any one quality be pursued to perfection. Perfecting one virtue means perfecting all virtue, as in normal physical growth a child's limbs grow simultaneously, not one after the other.

Those who successfully practise the martial arts present a broad outlook. They strive to inspire others through their own example, this being the soundest witness to the efficacy of their "way." By inspiring others to become all that they are capable of becoming, they constantly reinforce the spirit of the martial arts. By going outside of themselves to help others act likewise, their example can be emulated by practitioners and non-practitioners alike.

In our far-from Utopian society it is obvious that automation plays down the value of human labor. While people complain of the depersonalization wrought by mechanization, they are caught in the system that makes material prosperity depend on participation in a consumer-oriented society. Conservation is made to seem obsolete and self-destructive. To reduce personhood to a machine is to destroy the person. Machines serving man is good; but machines in preference to human welfare is unacceptable.

The martial arts make successful action depend on the continuous study and development of man. This idea has been supported through the ages by writers, historians, and inventors.

> *Know then thyself; presume not God to scan.*
> *The proper study of mankind is man.*[5]

The historian, Collingwood, says in his *The Idea of History:*

> *It is generally thought to be of importance to man that he*
> *should know himself...Knowing yourself means knowing first,*
> *what it is to be a man; secondly, knowing what it is to be the*
> *man you are and nobody else. Knowing yourself means*
> *knowing what you can do; and since nobody knows what he*
> *can do until he tries, the only clue to what man can do is what*
> *man has done.*[6]

In focusing attention on the objective study of man's nature and his life on earth, people carry on the Renaissance tradition of exalting the dignity of man. Not mere machines, men's lives are not determined by the arrangement and operation of atoms.

The strange and sometimes bitter miracle of life is nowhere more evident than in one's youth. Thomas Wolfe in *Man's Youth* expresses this idea.

> *(It is) that being rich, we are so poor; that being mighty, we*
> *can yet have nothing; that seeing, breathing, smelling, tasting*
> *all around us the impossible wealth and glory of this earth,*
> *feeling with an intolerable certitude that the whole structure of*
> *the enchanted life—the most fortunate, wealthy, good, and*
> *happy life that any man has ever known—is ours, at once, im-*
> *mediately and forever, the moment that we choose to take a*
> *step, or stretch a hand, or say a word, we yet know that we*
> *can really keep, hold, take, and possess forever—nothing.*[7]

Inherent to life are these paradoxes. In coping with them one must learn to cope with inherent contradictions as well. One is both great and helpless, destined for both glory and wretchedness, simultaneously endowed with reason and driven by an irrational life force. To withdraw from effort, however, is to withdraw from life.

The martial artist sees life as a matter of time rather than of space; a matter of change rather than of static presence; a fluid and persistent creation, not a quantity, not a mere redistribution of matter and motion. In order to understand the phenomenon of life, one must constantly examine that inner reality, oneself, with which one should be more familiar than with anything else. Introspection affects mind, not matter; action, not passivity; choice, not whim. This happens not in a vacuous mind, not in devitalized and separated parts, as when the biologist minutely studies the life systems of a dead specimen. It does happen with direct perception, simple and steady reflection, intuition, the most direct encounters possible to the human being.

Great people of the past dared to be "individuals;" they were not afraid to be themselves, letting even their weaknesses be known. In spite of them, they made their indelible mark on the pages of time. Milton in his blindness still wrote *Paradise Lost*, though he asked himself: "Does God exact day-labor, light denied?" and had the answer: "They serve best who do the best they can with what they are." Beethoven, stricken with deafness, continued to compose musical masterpieces. Yet he had his doubts, as indicated in a letter to his brother: "I must live like an exile. When I do venture near some social gathering, I am seized with a burning terror, the fear that I may be placed in a dangerous position of having to reveal my condition...Patience—so I am told, it is patience that I must now choose to be my guide: I have patience enough. My determination to hold out until it pleases the inexorable Fates to cut the thread shall be a lasting one, I sincerely hope...I am prepared."

Such examples epitomize the martial arts in action: being prepared for any eventuality, insignificant or critical; life, not necessarily filled with sound and fury, but certainly signifying something.

NOTES TO CHAPTER 9

1. *Aristotle, Nichomachean Ethics* translated by Martin Ostwald (The Bobbs-Merrill Co., 1962), p. 43.
2. Confucius, Sacred books of Confucius and other Confucius classics edited and translated by Ch'u Chai and Winberg Chai (University Books, New Hyde Park, New York, 1965), pp. 317-318.
3. Aristotle (op. cit.), pp. 95-97.
4. *Sources of Indian Tradition* edited by W. T. DeBary (Columbia University Press, New York, 1958), p. 33.
5. Alexander Pope, *Essays on Han in Tradition and Revolt* (Scott, Forseman and Co., New Jersey, 1951), p. 49.
6. Robin George Collingwood, *The Idea of History, Barden Lectures.* Written in 1936 On the Philosophy of History (Clarendon Press, Oxford, 1946), p. 10.
7. Thomas Wolfe, *Of Time and the River.* A legend of Man's Hunger in His Youth (Charles Scribner's Sons, New York, 1935), p. 454.

Chapter **10**

THE MARTIAL ARTS: ROAD TO DESTINY

"What is REAL?" asked the Rabbit...
"Real isn't how you are made," said the Skin Horse,
"It's a thing that happens to you. When a child loves you
for a long time, not just to play with, but really loves you,
then you become Real."
"Does it hurt?" asked the Rabbit.
"Sometimes," said the Skin Horse, for he was always
truthful. "When you are Real you don't mind being hurt."
"Does it happen all at once, like being wound up," he
asked, "or bit by bit?"
"It doesn't happen all at once," said the Skin Horse.
"You become. It takes a long time. That's why it doesn't
often happen to people who break easily, or have sharp
edges, or who have to be carefully kept. Generally, by the
time you are Real, most of your hair has been loved off,
and your eyes drop out and you get loose in the joints and
very shabby. But these things don't matter at all, because
once you are Real you can't be ugly, except to people who
don't understand."
—The Velveteen Rabbit

In the martial arts the person is seen as an active agent. He is an entity that can claim, I am myself and nobody else; I exist continuously until I die. I possess certain inalienable qualities which make me substantial and unique." To claim agency is to confirm that one assumes responsibility to defend one's self, to preserve substantiality in order to fulfill one's part in society. Theory is uselsss unless it leads to effective action, bringing the martial artist to follow a most productive and successful life.

In order to reach this point, one's self-knowledge must be characterized in ability, desire, and duty. A person who does this knows what he wants to do, what he can do, and what he ought to do. He does not desire what is impossible, but he does what he ought, because what he ought encompasses both what he wants to do and what he can do.

Such knowledge begins with the person but does not stay there. It extends to society for two reasons: others teach one a great deal about oneself; and one must learn one's position in the social perspective, with its mutually inherent responsibilities.

The universe contains many unexplained phenomena. However, the more man discovers, the more there is to discover. Most active in the discovering process is reason—always leaving room for inspiration, of course. While conscientiously performing all the tasks nature has imposed on him, the martial artist calls on his self-reliance to keep rationality at the helm. In his life's quest he will free himself from the desires that blind the eye of reason and obscure the "way."

In both act and speech the martial artist asserts a humble but secure self-profile that makes others comfortable in his presence, for he evinces a benign authority. A deficiency in one's decision-making ability can ruin all this. It can lead to ludicrous, if not serious, results. Aesop's tale provides a typical example.

> A miller and his young son were on their way to market to sell a donkey. Soon some people by the way remarked:
> "Look at the silly pair, walking in the dust when they could be riding in comfort on the beast's back."
> Hearing this, the old man mounted the donkey with his son, and rode on. Hardly had they gone a few meters when another group of onlookers remarked:
> "Look at that lazy pair of brutes, breaking the back of that poor animal."
> Again the old man heard, and immediately descended, letting the boy continue to ride. But soon he heard yet another judgment:
> "What a disrespectful boy! He rides while his old father has to walk." At this the old man changed places with his son. Hardly had he done so when some old ladies protested:
> "What a mean old man! He rides while the child must struggle to keep up on foot." Once more the old man descended, but just then heard some merchants say:
> "How worn-out that donkey looks! He will not fetch a penny for his owner." So the man and his son slung the donkey on a pole between them, and began to carry him over a bridge. The donkey struggled to get loose, fell down, and drowned in the river. Thus, by trying to please everyone, the miller pleased no one and lost his donkey besides. [1]

The miller's problem was clearly a lack of self-confidence. A self-reliant person need not worry about what people say because he knows what he can do. Besides, opinions cannot make one either better or worse than one actually is. Therefore, as long as one has not compromised on one's best effort, one will never fail even though an undertaking may not turn out as expected. Greatness lies in retaining one's initiative despite "failures."

> *If you can keep your head when all about you*
> *Are losing theirs and blaming it on you, ...*
> *If you can bear to hear the truth you've spoken*
> *Twisted by knaves to make a trap for fools,*
> *Or watch the things you gave your life to, broken,*
> *And stoop and build 'em up with worn-out tools, ...*
> *If neither foes nor loving friends can hurt you,*
> *If all men count with you, but none too much; ...*
> *Yours is the Earth and everything that's in it,*
> *And—which is more—you'll be a Man, my son!* [2]

Greek literature also offers an example of the type of detachment from materialism and human respect held up by the martial artist for imitation.

> *According to legend, Diogenes slept in a tub in the open air, carried food in a wallet, and was not ashamed to beg alms. Even his begging was unconventional. "My friend," he once said to a miserly man who was slow to respond, "it's for food I want, not funeral expenses."*
> *On another occasion he was found begging alms of a statue, "in order," he said, "to get practice in being refused."*
> *By the time Alexander had ascended the throne of Macedon, the fame of Diogenes, then some seventy years old, had spread throughout Greece. One day, as the old philosopher lay sunning himself in his tub, Alexander rode up with his retinue. Drawing rein in front of the tub, he announced: "I am Alexander the Great."*
> *"And I," replied the other composedly, "am Diogenes the Dog."*
> *"Are you not afraid of me?" Alexander asked.*
> *"Why, what are you, something good or something evil?"*
> *"Something good, of course."*
> *"Well," retorted Diogenes, "who would be so foolish as to fear anything good?"*
> *Struck with admiration for this answer, Alexander exclaimed, "Ask anything you wish of me, and I will grant it."*
> *"Then be so kind," said Diogenes, "as to get out of my sunlight."* [3]

With conviction, one has no fear; without it, one has no hope.

In life the individual not only acts: he is acted upon. How he responds to this external power is an important element in his development. In this the martial arts have adopted a fundamental principle from Taoism. It is illustrated in the "actionless action" of water, the weak and unresisting element which bypasses the opposing rock, yet eventually makes it crumble. This features the supremacy of unassertiveness, of gentleness. Concomitant with this principle is the renunciation of violence and aggression. Death, too, is gentle and natural.

> *O the great way o'erflows*
> *And spreads on every side!*
> *All being comes from it;*
> *No creature is denied.*
> *But having called them forth,*
> *It calls not one its own.*
> *It feeds and clothes them all*
> *And will not be their lord.*
> *Without desire always,*
> *It seems of slight import.*
> *Yet, nonetheless, in this*
> *Its greatness still appears:*
> *When they return to it,*
> *No creatures meets a lord.*
>
> *The Wise Man, therefore, while he is alive,*
> *Will never make a show of being great:*
> *And that is how his greatness is achieved.* [4]

The martial artist is able through self-mastery indirectly to control his environment, for he decides how much he will allow it to affect him. In being master of himself he is less a victim to circumstance. Instead, he is an active force in what goes on in his world. Every detail of the martial artist's life is maintained in the perspective of his self-knowledge. He is not the miller in Aesop's fable who does not know what to do with his donkey. Rather, like Diogenes, he is confident whether cynic or king. He knows in his heart the readiness advised by the Duke to Claudio in *Measure for Measure:*

> *Be absolute for death; either death or life*
> *Shall thereby be the sweeter. Reason thus with life:*

If I do lose thee, I do lose a thing
That none but fools would keep. A breath thou art,
Servile to all the skyey influences,
That doest this habitation where thou keep'st
Hourly afflict. [5]

The way is not easily followed without persistence. The martial artist is aware of the thin line between success and failure. While one drop of water carries next to no power by itself, a continuous chain of drops splits the rock. Patient persistence is the art of devoting relentless effort to a project until it is successfully completed. Just as nature arranges the way of water, so the world makes way for a man who knows where he is going.

Both life and the martial arts have in common that each has a unified goal. By bringing together many disciplines into one, seemingly impossible feats can be effected. This is done through developing correct techniques emanating from right attitudes. Only through coordinating mind and body can proper focus be achieved. This, of course, goes beyond external acts, for personal integrity and persevering determination are essential to the art in which observing, thinking, and doing become practically synonymous.

A key ingredient in perfect technique is timing. One cannot survive in competitive society if one passes up too many chances. In the martial arts timing is the cement that binds all the other elements together. To say, for instance, that a punch has been delivered too early or too late is to say that the punch was futile.

Whatever you can do, or dream you can, begin it.
Boldness has genius, power and magic in it. [6]

The martial arts teach this kind of "boldness." Threats to one's future destiny must be overcome before there can be any chance for free action. The enemies of future security and success are not so much environment as they are the emotional states that interfere with the functioning of mind and body.

In this respect the martial arts are quite different from sport. While the baseball player, for instance, may condition himself by practice swings and warm-ups, there comes the moment at the plate when practice is over and an error is irretrievable. Should the batter miss a decisive play, however, he can always make it up in the next game. This is not so in the martial arts. There are no "practice swings" beforehand, since one can never be sure what an opponent will do until he does it. What is more, no two opponents will do the same thing in similar circumstances. The defender has one instant only to respond correctly; failure in that instant is total failure. This is likewise true of many chances life offers.

> There is a tide in the affairs of men
> Which, taken at the flood, leads on to fortune;
> Omitted, all the voyage of their life
> Is bound in shallows and in miseries. [7]

Once one is master of the focus within, then success, happiness and spiritual serenity are secure on every level.

The martial arts are, indeed, arts of self-defense; but they are more. They are the means to the end. The progression of self-improvement begins with self-knowledge, defining what one can and ought to do. This inspires confidence and control, which in turn bring harmonious action within a given environment, resulting in a sense of achievement and success.

NOTES TO CHAPTER 10

1. Charles W. Eliot, Editor. *The Harvard Classics* (P.F. Collier & Son Company, New York, 1909), Vol. 17, p. 36.
2. Rudyard Kipling "IF" Rudyard Kipling's Verse, Definitive Edition (Doubleday and Company, Inc., Garden City, New York, 1940), p. 578.
3. Will Durant, *The Mensions of Philosophy* (Simon and Schuster, New York, 1929), p. 485.
4. Lao Tzu, Tao Te Ching 34.
5. Shakespeare, *Measure for Measure, Act III, Scene I.,* Complete Signet Classic, Shakespeare (Harcourt Brace Johanovich, Inc., New York, 1976), p. 1156.
6. Johann W. Von Goethe, Faust, Essays on Han in Tradition and Revolt (Scott, Forseman and Co., New Jersey, 1951), p. 476.
7. Julius Caesar, *The Tragedy of Julius Caesar* (The Yale Shakespeare) Ed. Lawrence Mason (Yale University Press, New Haven, 1957), p. 79.

Chapter **11**

MEDITATION, CONCENTRATION, FOCUS IN THE MARTIAL ARTS

I Ching is the interplay of the polar opposites yin and yang. The yang is represented by a solid line (____), the yin by a broken line (__ __), and the whole system of hexagrams is built up naturally from these two lines. By adding a third line to each pair, eight "trigrams" and generated (as illustrated in the epigram).
                                                    —I Ching

Life can only be understood backwards,
but must be lived forwards.
                                    —S. Kierkegaard

The unexamined life is not worth living.
                                    —Socrates

The world's best thinkers used and advocated the practice of meditation as necessary to the influx of spiritual energy and the elevation of the soul to God. The purpose of looking inward is to enlarge one's capacity to tap one's own deeper levels of insight, ethical sensitivity and awareness, in which tradition and immediate experience are not opposed to each other but inter-related.[1] One cannot reach these deeper levels in a flurry of activities, amidst the pressures and constant distractions of everyday life. Therefore, it behooves one to withdraw into the inner cell of self to discover and/or re-affirm that clear explanation of life that every individual needs, in the light of an intelligible theory or belief.[2]

Meditation can be prolonged over several days or it may be as short as a few minutes. Because the martial arts involve physical as well as mental activity, they advocate a combination of prolonged and shortened meditative practices. Solitude for a few days is taken up as an annual exercise, during which the individual examines his life wholly and in detail, striving to strengthen the ethical spirit while re-conditioning the letter of the law. Having done this conscientiously, it takes only a few intense minutes daily to recall and recapture what was then set out, and so hold faithfully to the way of the martial arts. "In the Socratic view," writes Kierkegaard, "each individual is his own center, and the entire world centers in him, because his self-knowledge is a knowledge of God."[3]

There are many ways of meditating, but most have certain features in common. An exterior pre-condition to successful meditation is to be in a quiet place, alone, and undisturbed. An interior pre-condition is for the individual to be relaxed but not tired, to be neither over-fed nor hungry, to be naturally free from alcohol and drugs. Cleanliness and loose-fitting clothing are also helpful. One may assume any suitable posture: walking, sitting, reclining, gently rocking—whatever is conducive to stimulating the thought process. A posture most frequently adopted is sitting on a cushion, the back of which is slightly higher than the front. The person does not rest his back against any support; he crosses his legs, the sole of each foot placed upward on the thigh of the other leg. His hands are placed easily one above the other. Ears and shoulders remain horizontally parallel; nose and navel are vertically in the same plane. He keeps his mouth closed and breathes through his nose. The energy of the entire body is concentrated on the lower abdomen (which is important to correct breathing). He keeps his eyes open, and fixed at a distance of two to three feet in front of him. If the person feels unusually refreshed, he may close his eyes. He remains thus for whatever time he has set; when finished, he rises slowly and quietly.

This serenity becomes habitual even in the midst of intense, perhaps nerve-wracking activity. The mind is cleared of resentments, aversions, and unnecessary distractions; it remains open, alert, refreshed. So, the effects of meditation are carried into action: mind and body flow in the same direction. Thus, the eye serves the sense of sight, but the mind provides perception, even as a window lets in light but is not the light.

Different cultures produce different approaches to this kind of reflection. A widely used practice is East Indian yoga, the state of consciousness induced by the successful exercise of concentration.

When we control mental restlessness, we are able to see what should be seen. And by controlling physical restlessness, we have more energy to do what should be done.

As we sit quietly and concentrate inwardly, we experience ourselves *directly. This experience unfolds for us a greater awareness of ourselves and our place in the world. It can be quite a discovery!*[4]

{ Since mind and body are inseparable, yoga is used to develop and discipline both by exercising them simultaneously. }

Ƨ Meditation, contemplation, reflection: these set the stage to effective physical action. In its more detailed application, it becomes concentration. ʂ

II

The instruction given to swordsmen by the great fencing master, Takuan, elucidates this Zen contribution to the martial arts.

> *What is most important is to acquire a certain mental attitude known as 'immovable wisdom.' The wisdom is intuitively acquired after a great deal of practical training. You must follow the movement...of the opponent, leaving your mind free to make its own countermovement without your interfering deliberation. You move as the opponent moves, and it will result in his own defeat.*[5]

Ɛ The martial arts term applied to this type of concentration is "mushim"—literally, "no-mind." It allows conscious acts to be performed unconsciously Ɛ Everyday life provides ready examples of this. A skilled car driver "automatically" stops for a red light; he "automatically" shifts gears, uses the brake, gives signals. He may be carrying on a lively conversation all the while that he is doing these other things. This habituation of appropriate action is a *sine qua non* in the martial arts. To have to stop to think when one should be acting is death to smooth functioning. Self-consciousness, symptomized by one's desire to impress through a display in skill or the obsession to be victor at whatever cost, seriously interferes with one's performance and will freeze the action. The ability to concentrate corrects the tendency of the mind to diffuseness, and instead, fixes it on a single "action," excluding all others.

The acquisition of the techniques of the martial arts requires this kind of concentration. To achieve it successfully, the techniques must be sufficiently developed to inspire confidence. It may be thought that there is no great need to perfect concentration during training because "rational" beings will naturally behave "rationally." But there is a fine distinction between rationality and purpose. It is all too easy to forget purpose and principles while in the melee of activity, neglecting even the most obvious advantage. This is not necessarily due to rashness or passion; it is a matter of neglect in concentration.

When an individual converts concentration into action, the movement is called focus. A vitalized mental image becomes a physical reality. The combination of concentration and focus intensifies power two-, four-, tenfold. Through training, all mental activities can be brought under the habitual control (more or less) of the will. Worry, anxiety, anger and other negative emotions can be kept in check.

The martial arts relate concentration to Oriental philosophy whose main emphasis is mental and moral superiority. Self-understanding and self-reliance are basic to this. "For the mind," said Arjuna, "is verily restless, O Krishna: it is impetuous, strong, and difficult to bend. I deem it as hard to curb as the wind." Krishna answered, "It may be curbed by constant practice and by indifference (dispassion)."

Socrates' example shows the value he laid on clear thinking. Plato in the *Symposium* recounts the following incident:

> *One morning he was thinking about something which he could not resolve. He would not give it up, but continued thinking from early dawn until noon—there he stood fixed in thought and at noon attention was drawn to him, and the rumor ran through the wondering crowd that Socrates had been standing and thinking about something ever since the break of day. At last, in the evening after supper, some Ionians out of curiosity, brought out their mats and slept in the open air that they might watch him and see whether he would stand all night. There he stood until the following morning and with the return of light he offered up a prayer to the sun and went his way.*[6]

Elsewhere the *Symposium* relates that Socrates had "a way of stopping anywhere and losing himself" in thought.

Zen Buddhism suggests a way adopted by the martial arts for achieving concentration; that is the direct method of illuminating action. Without its spirit—the realization of the absolute oneness of things—physical power is largely wasted. The objective on a physical level is always minimum output of energy for maximum return of power. On the other hand, concentration is ineffectual without direct action. Thus, the method of informed action is applied in the martial arts.

III

Physical concentration—that is, focus—is the practical outcome of mental concentration. Proper focus is achieved in two ways. One is to co-ordinate every body muscle to focus on one point. This is especially relevant for the use of larger muscles in the hips and abdomen. The second is to transfer this mobilized action to the smallest possible area. There must be no waste of power. That is the key to full-force delivery in attack or defense.

Conscious action is slow and accurate. Subconscious action is fast and unpredictable. In the martial arts the individual practises concentration to the point where conscious and subconscious work together for perfect execution of action. Basic routines are so engrained that free-sparring is fully controlled. In the training hall practitioners make only light contact, if any. This takes deeper concentration and sharper focus than the all-out emergency attack in a life-or-death situation.

The high strength factor in the martial arts is the result of concerted training in concentration. The practitioner conserves energy so that he has it to release at exactly the time, in exactly the place it is needed. The release occurs not only during a fight, but it happens any time the individual engages in effective work; that is, in creativity. In ch'i (or *ki*) the principle of differentiation and individuation, all that has physical form is identifiable with the vital force. When anything disintegrates, its vital force is at an end and a new entity appears. In modern physics this is called the principle of novelty in creation or transformation; energy can be neither created nor destroyed, merely changed. Lao-tzu notes figuratively the "slippery" nature of the nameless (force, energy) of the Tao:

> *We gaze at it but see it not; it is called invisible.*
> *We listen to it but hear it not; it is call inaudible.*
> *We grasp it but find it not; it is called intangible.*
> *These three all elude our inquiries, and hence*
>   *merge into One.*
> *Its rising brings no light; its sinking, no darkness.*
> *Continuous, unceasing, and unnameable, it returns*
>   *to no (particular) thingness.*
> *This is called the formless form, the imageless image.*
> *This is called the vague and elusive.*
> *We meet it and do not see its face;*
> *We follow it and do not see its back.*[7]

He also describes energy as the fundamental basis of the universe, regarding Tao as the basic principle of its transformation:

> *Tao produced One; One produces Two;*
> *Two produces Three; Three produces all things.*
> *All things carry the yin and embrace the yang,*
> *And attain their harmony through the proper blending*
>   *of ch'i (energy).*[8]

To know the theories of potential, kinetic, and heat energies is one thing; to acquire the skills to change one form to another with maximum efficiency is another—much more difficult to accomplish. It is precisely here that the expert reaps the fruit of meditation, concentration, and focus. Say, the end desired were a knockout blow. Working backwards, the kinetic energy released would not have been possible before the potential energy for it existed. The potential energy resided within the "agent:" in his mind and body. Yet, the only way he could transform his "potential" to "actual" without wasting heat energy would be through proper motivation (by meditation) to effectively decide on the release of energy (by concentration) to a sharply defined target (focus). The combination of confidence, born of meditation and knowledge of self, along with refined concentration and expert focus comes only with countless hours of guided practice in technique. Thus, energy at rest means that all muscles, tendons, and nerves, when not in use, remain loose and relaxed so that there may be instant and full response to any new set of stimuli. If the energizers (muscles et al) are already tense before action, they cannot be further tensed at the time of focus, and so inefficiency is the result. The practitioner learns to coordinate the stronger but slower-to-react muscles in hips and abdomen, with the weaker but faster-to-react muscles (tendons) in feet and hands, to focus on the smallest possible target or vital spot. Keen focus will always win over sheer brute force.

≶ Mind and body are but two aspects of the one reality: energy. One informs the other. The "informing" is found in the combined exercise of meditation flowing into concentration flowing into focus. This is the martial arts' *ch'i.* ≶

NOTES TO CHAPTER 11
1. Rollo May. *Man's Search for Himself,* (W.W. Norton Company: 1953), p. 184.
2. Henry W. Maier. *Three Theories of Child Development,* (New York, Harper and Row: 1965), p. 26.
3. Roll May, *Ibid.,* p. 190.
4. Michaeline Kiss. *Yoga for Young People,* (Archway Paperback: 1973), flypage.
5. D.T. Suzuki, *Zen Buddhism,* (New York: 1959), pp. 291-292.
6. Plato, The Works of Plato, translated by B. Jewett Vol. III (Tudor Publishing Company, New York), p. 297, p. 354.
7. Lao Tzu, Tao Te Ching, p. 14.
8. Ibid., p. 42.

Chapter **12**

THE MARTIAL ARTS AND HEALTH

By health I mean the power to live a full, adult, living,
    breathing life in close contact with what I love—
the earth and the wonders thereof—the sea, the sun.
    All that we mean when we speak of the eternal world.
    ...
I want to be all that I am capable of becoming so that I
    may be a child in the sun.
                                    —Katharine Mansfield

Having said so much about mind and spirit, one might wonder by now just where the physical stands in the scheme of the martial arts. The answer is unequivocal: the body is the partner, the companion, the co-worker of the mind. It is the tangible instrument of intangible reality, and deserves the greatest respect. The martial arts' goal is *total* health, and that is complete only if the body, too, is at its best.

Daily headlines blare out imminent threats to health: pollution of air, water, and sound; nuclear fall-out and radiation; cancer-producing foods; psychological warfare and the moral pollutants of prejudice, corruption, and child abuse. Perhaps the individual feels helpless to turn the tide against so many ills, but there is nothing wrong with starting on *one:* himself. It may be more difficult to achieve success in this matter in the Western system than in the Oriental, given that the former concentrates on remedies (control by bacterial experimentation, medicine, drugs) as contrasted to the latter's emphasis on prevention through natural means (correct eating, abdominal breathing and exercise, the use of herbs, acupuncture). However, it is by no means impossible wherever one may be.

As for a program of health and fitness: there are many good books on the market today, any one of which will outline such a program. A basic knowledge of anatomy is also necessary. There is no intention of going into every aspect of these subjects here, as the martial arts subscribe to current medical and dietary common sense from a reputable source. However, those features more directly affecting the practice of the martial arts will be the subject of some detailed consideration. Among these are breathing, rhythm, and equilibrium.

Longevity is no great feat if it is but a vegetable existence. Given equality in all other respects, a short, full life is preferable to a long, empty existence. High achievement is not necessarily the result of being better equipped, but more of being firmly determined. The practitioner boldly seizes the opportunities at hand and makes the most of them. Health is not a matter of bulging muscles. Comparing the achievement of a weight lifter or a wrestler to that of a martial artist, one would see the difference in the effect of brute force and that of focal projection. The martial artist is more akin to the master of dance than to the boxing champion.

In judo, for example, the practitioner uses the weight and strength of his opponent for the opponent's own undoing. The judo expert may be less "healthy" than his opponent, but he is more "fit" in that his preparation necessarily included a knowledge of health and anatomy. How else could he know the body's vital spots, the nerves, the glands to immobilize in temporary paralysis? How could he know exactly how much force to use, and exactly where to apply it? His moral integrity as well prescribes only immobilization of his opponent, not a killing; he is to use pain as a deterrent rather than destruction.

So the body must be kept as a finely tuned instrument. The centre of tuning is, of course, the brain. It is said to be the most complex structure in the universe. Within its three pounds are one thousand billion protein molecules, used to file away every sight, sound, taste, smell, action, experience, thought, and fantasy. Throughout the body it has some 500,000 assistant touch detectors, and more than 200 temperature detectors. No computer or radar centre has come near the brain's capacity to detect, motivate, adjust, and control. Therefore, it is of paramount importance to keep the brain functioning at its constant best.

Attitudes to life and one's self-profile have already been discussed in connection to performance. A further word on stress is appropriate. Stress has always been around and is not all bad; it differs in degree from the caveman's worry whether he would eat or be eaten, to today's concern about inflation and the neutron bomb. Dr. Hans Selye, a Montreal physician, uses the term "eustress' for the pleasant kind (such as that experienced in successful writing, athletic competition, or conducting a symphony orchestra); and "distress" to signify the unhealthy kind (such as anxiety, fear, resentment). Under stress of either kind certain chemical and physical reactions occur: the endocrines, such as the pituitary gland located just under the brain, produce a hormone which, in turn, stimulates the adrenal glands which, in turn, produce adrenalin—that sudden burst of energy that comes up in emergencies. All demands, whether on the brain, liver, muscles, or bones, cause stress, even under deep anesthesia, an emotionless state. Blood pressure, hormone levels, and the electric activity of the brain are all affected. Pulse rate increases, sweat glands are activated, all nerve centres are put on immediate alert.

To the question, "What are the more frequent causes of distress?", Dr. Selye replies:

> *One cannot generalize. They differ in various civilizations and historical periods. At certain times, pestilence and hunger were the predominant causes. Another, then and now, is warfare or the fear of war.*
>
> *At the moment (1977), I would say the most frequent causes of distress in man are psychological—that is to say, lack of adaptability,* not having a code of behavior. *One reason for this is that the satisfaction of religious codes has diminished in importance for mankind. So has the idea of being loyal to your monarch or leader. Even the satisfaction of accumulating dollars has been diminished by inflation.*
>
> *The problem was well expressed four centuries ago by my favorite French author, Montaigne, who said, 'No wind blows in favor of the ship that has no port of destination.'*[1]

"Not having a code of behavior," (the italics have been added) sums up the entire statement. This is exactly what the martial arts provide: a code of behavior, having *a way of life*. It seems that people today are so busy making a living, they have no time to live.

Physical activity almost certainly is one way to relieve distress,[2] as chronic exposure to undue pressures can cause serious illnesses: heart attack, nervous breakdown, high blood pressure, ulcers, psychosomatic disorders. Since one cannot engage in every kind of exercise, one must determine intelligently what one needs, and then choose accordingly. The martial arts recommend jogging, cycling, swimming as therapeutic in that they produce longer, more resilient muscles as opposed to short, lumpy ones produced by isotonics. The former involve larger body areas and are more beneficial to cardio-vascular and respiratory systems.

This leads into a consideration of the importance of breathing. Ordinarily, the autonomous nervous system manages shallow breathing, but this can and should be extended. For instance, during normal, effortless breathing, one can deliberately concentrate on what is actually happening as one breathes in and breathes out. One tries to forget all else for the moment. It is advisable, to eliminate distraction, to keep the eyes downcast, and to become fully aware of just breathing. The exercise may be practised usefully for as long as seems comfortable or as time permits.

There is a special kind of breathing that is particularly recommended to calm the emotions, quiet the mind, regulate the circulation, and mobilize joints, ligaments, and muscles. This breathing is mentally directed to sink to the *danjeon,* or hypogastric region (about three inches below the navel), during both inhalation and exhalation. It is done slowly and quietly. The contraction and expansion of abdominal muscles alternates the abdominal pressure. When the pressure is high, the abdominal veins carry blood to the right side of the heart; when the pressure is relieved, the blood circulates again to the abdomen. While aiding circulation, this also, for instance, massages the liver.

The mechanisms of the caudal brain stem assist danjeon breathing. The contraction of the thoracic and abdominal musculature expands the chest cavity and draws air into the lungs. This is initiated by lower brain stem neurons, the efferent fibres of which descend to the spinal outflows of the inspiratory muscles. These brain stem neurons are continuously excited by many factors related to oxygen deficiency. The active contraction of expiratory muscles is added to the relaxation of inspiratory ones in exhaling air during danjeon breathing.

In the martial arts breathing is inseparable from the idea of rhythm. Again, yoga offers a practical illustration, for in it all movements are made slowly and rhythmically into and out of a posture

or pose. The mind is concentrated on the movements of the body during
the physical exercise, and on the stillness of the body during hold. Deep
breathing is used within each exercise to help establish an easy rhythm to
avoid unnatural strain. The tempo of any exercise is always rhythmic
and orderly.[3]

"Orderly" means harmonious co-ordination in the martial arts.
Thus, the transition from mental to physical set is smooth and flowing.
This continuous flow passes into all the physical routines on the training
floor (and into everyday activities). The tempo may vary as the situations vary, but a basic rhythm flows through all.

Suzanne K. Langer calls rhythm "the most characteristic principle
of vital activity. All life is rhythmic," she points out; under difficult circumstances, the rhythm may be very complex, but when these rhythms
are lost life cannot long endure.[4] The cycle of the seasons, the orbiting
of the planets, the rotation of the earth, the alternations of growth and
decay, of birth and death, the beating of the heart: all life and activity
pulse in rhythm. Even society entertains a certain rhythm, for on the sea
of life, it undulates with cosmic forces, as in times of natural giving
(food, light, air, water) and taking (famine, floods, fires, tornadoes).
Civilizations have risen and died on their capacity to roll with the waves
of change.

To look at a more practical application in the martial arts, body
rhythms vary in their demands both as to intensity and as to speed. Increased physical activity demands an increase of oxygen intake, signaled
by more rapid breathing and heartbeat. Mountain climbers have observed that high altitudes slow down mental activity and diminish the
power to think clearly. Sustained high altitude residence requires
habitually deeper breathing; body form is altered (the chest becoming
more barrel-shaped), and the skin color becomes darker and redder.
The hemoglobin content in the blood increases, making the blood
"thicker" because of the increase of red corpuscles. Such blood takes
greater energy to circulate and could cause heart problems. Too sudden
a change in such atmospheric pressure causes severe pain (as air pilots
can attest), even lapses into unconsciousness. The principle of ch'i,
already mentioned in a previous chapter, enters perfectly into this
rhythm.[5]

The ch'i condenses and disperses rhythmically, bringing forth
all forms which eventually dissolve into the void. The Great
Void cannot but consist of ch'i; this ch'i cannot but condense
to form all things; and these things cannot but become dis-
persed so as to form (once more) the Great Void.

All of this has to do with maintaining a proper balance between supply and demand. This defines the martial arts' use of the term *equilibrium.* A time of activity must be succeeded by a time of rest, the trough must succeed the crest, darkness the light, the dry the wet, and so on. One recalls the principle of yin and yang (see Chapter 4). The dynamic nature of the balanced interplay integral to this principle and central to all phenomena is further set out in the *I Ching* (Book of Changes).

The Changes is a book
From which one may not hold aloof.
Its tao is forever changing—
Alteration, movement without rest,
Flowing through the six empty places,
Rising and sinking without fixed law,
Firm and yielding transform each other.
They cannot be confined within a rule,
It is only change that is at work here.[6]

More than any other, the philosophy of yin and yang put Oriental and social teaching on a cosmological basis. Its ideas affect every aspect of life from metaphysics to art, from marriage to cooking stew. That is why it fits so well into the martial arts program. Wherever harmony is sought or change takes place, the forces of yin and yang are at work. This embodies the concept of equilibrium, the opposing and complementary principles regulating the motions of the universe. So modern a writer as Bertrand Russell expressed the same idea.

It aims only at clarifying the fundamental ideas of the sciences,
and synthesizing the different sciences in a single comprehensive
view of that fragment of the world that science has succeeded in
exploring. It does not know what lies beyond; it possesses no talis-
man for transforming ignorance into knowledge. It offers intellec-
tual delights to those who value them, but it does not attempt to
flatter human conceit as most philosophies do. If it is dry and
technical, it lays the blame on the universe, which has chosen to
work in a mathematical way rather than as poets or mystics might
have desired.[7]

Personal equilibrium is understood through and reflected in the individual's attitudes toward himself and others. Social psychology, according to Heider's theory, involves identifying states of balance and imbalance in the cognitive system of an experiencing person as he entertains specified relationships with other persons and with attitudinal objects. The relationship between the experiencing person, the object, and another person are all in equilibrium when all three relations are positive or when one is positive and two are negative. Imbalance occurs when two of them are positive and the other negative.

How is this exemplified in the martial arts? Suppose a student is sparring with a partner who loses his temper, and his sparring becomes ruthless. An unhealthy tension develops. The "dislike" of the ruthless partner is bent on destruction, and this is negative; the balance in the triad of student, opponent, and art is destroyed. The impulse to "destroy" is false to the spirit of the martial arts; every motion must be for preservation, not revenge. An opponent is not kicked for personal satisfaction.

Social equilibrium, necessary for effectively playing one's role in society, is established and maintained through respect for others and adherence to rules of propriety. One is aware not only of one's own shortcomings, but learns to recognize these in others; coping with these is twofold: trying to modify oneself or another reasonably, and tolerating or abandoning those elements that are beyond one's ability to change.

The physically direct application of equilibrium in the gymnasium means a firm stance; an individual will not be toppled by an attacker, and also have a firm foundation from which to launch a forceful attack. Static (bracing) and dynamic (moving) balance can be thought of separately only for purposes of discussion. One speaks of beginning, change, and follow-through in the process of effecting equilibrium. In practice, they are non-existent if separated. Static and dynamic balance *together*—and in no other way—bring maximum power.

Spelled out, balanced stance requires that the centre of gravity (weight) of the body fall on an imaginary vertical plane midway through the body, with weight equally distributed on both legs. If a shift in weight onto one foot is necessary, the centre of gravity should be in the centre of that foot. Often equilibrium of stance is aided by an accompanying rotation of the foot in prompt response to required change. A side stance, for example, begins with the front foot parallel to the direction one is facing. In the process of punching, the rear foot rotates to a position perpendicular to its original position so that at the completion of the movement, the toes of the rear foot are pointing forward. The hips and waist are simultaneously rotated in the same direction as the foot, while the non-punching arm and shoulder are jerked back for reaction force.

The same technique applies to kicking. For a front thrust kick, for example, the centre of gravity is shifted midway between the legs onto the centre of one foot, while a simultaneous back-thrust of the shoulders aids balance and force. In a side kick the base foot during action must turn in the same direction as the kicking foot. The heel of the rear foot never leaves the ground at the time of impact. Knee spring "links" the two pivotal forces of foot and hip, and acts as the mean for vertical equilibrium of body weight.

The intimate relationship of focus, rhythm, and equilibrium is clearly obvious: preparation, action, and follow-through are "energy" in its potential, kinetic, and heat forms, respectively. Power accumulated through acceleration is possible only by means of perfect balance among these elements.

The martial arts demand no less than total dedication. To become (and to remain) physically and mentally vigorous, the practitioner must devote as much time and thought to his energy balance sheet as a careful businessman gives to his operating budget. While illness and other forms of distress cannot be avoided or ignored, they can be organized and controlled. Working *with* life's rhythms, exercising danjeon breathing, correcting imbalances, provides more than enough energy to power the most demanding life-style. Co-ordinating one's daily biorhythms (biological and psychological cycles) can result only in improved human behavior and in personal fulfillment.

NOTES TO CHAPTER 12

1. U.S. News and World Report, 2300 N. St., N.W., Washington, D.C., March 21, 1977, from an interview with Hans Selye. Other ideas on stress in this section also agree with this source.

2. Practical examples are not hard to find. Take the case of someone coming home after a long day's work. She is "pooped" to exhaustion, physically and mentally. A fifteen-minute swim in the backyard pool brings her out refreshed, alert, toned, and ready for another eight hours' work.

3. Michaeline Kiss, *op. cit.,* p. 17. A more complete quotation clarifies the point. Deep Breathing is one of the most important Yoga exercises. Do it often. It circulates the new air in the body and expels the used air. It affects your complexion, your alertness, and even your feelings. If you are nervous, a long deep breath will calm you. Professional sportsmen poise themselves this way before shooting for a basket or kicking a ball.

   Use it to calm yourself before sports, before taking a test, or whenever you feel jittery. Use it also when you feel sluggish. Deep Breathing is nature's own equalizer. If the body is tired, it will perk it up. If the mind is anxious or upset, it will calm it down. Practise correct breathing until you can do it automatically.

4. Suzanne K. Langer. *Feeling and Form* (Charles Scribner Sons, New York: 1953), p. 126.

5. H. Weyl. *Philosophy of Mathematics and Natural Science* (Princeton University Press: 1949), p. 171.

6. Chuang-tzu, trans. James Legge (Ace Books, New York: 1971), p. 348. An explanation of the epigram of "lines" at the opening of this chapter is revealing. The following quotation comes from *The Tao of Physics* by Fritjof Capra (The Chaucer Press, Bungay, Suffolk: 1975), p. 294 ff. Chinese philosophy...which also emphasizes movement and change, has developed the notion of dynamic patterns which are continually formed and dissolved again in the cosmic flow of the *Tao*. In the *I Ching,* or Book of Changes, these patterns have been elaborated into a system of archetypal symbols, the so-called hexagrams.

   The basic ordering principle of the patterns in the *I Ching* is...the interplay of the polar opposites *yin* and *yang*. The yang is represented by a solid line(____), the yin by a broken line (__ __), and the whole system of hexagrams is built up naturally from these two lines. By adding a third line to each pair, eight 'trigrams' are generated (as illustrated in the epigram).

   In ancient China, the trigrams were considered to represent all possible cosmic and human situations. They were given names reflecting their basic characteristics—such as 'The Creative,' 'The Receptive,' 'The Arousing,' and so on—and they were associated with many images taken from nature and from social life. They represented, for example, heaven, earth, thunder, water, etc., as well as a family consisting of father, mother, three sons and three daughters. They were, furthermore, associated with the cardinal points and with the seasons of the year. ...

   In order to increase the number of possible combinations further, the eight trigrams were combined in pairs by placing one above the other. In this way, sixty-four hexagrams were obtained, each consising of six solid or broken lines. ...

   The sixty-four hexagrams are the cosmic archetypes on which the use of the *I Ching* as an oracle book is based. For the interpretation of any hexagram, the various meanings of its two trigrams have to be taken into account. For example, when the trigram 'The Arousing' is situated above the trigram 'The Receptive,' the hexagram is interpreted as movement meeting with devotion and thus inspiring enthusiasm, which is the name given to it.

NOTES TO CHAPTER 12

...The hexagram for Progress, to give another example, represents 'The Clinging' above 'The Receptive' which is interpreted as the sun rising over the earth and thus as a symbol of rapid, easy progress. ...

In the *I Ching,* the trigrams and hexagrams represent the patterns of the *Tao* which are generated by the dynamic interplay of the yin and the yang, and are reflected in all cosmic and human situations. These situations, therefore, are not seen as static, but rather as stages in a continuous flow and change. This is the basic idea of the Book of Changes which is expressed in its very title. All things and situations in the world are subject to change and transformation, and so are their images, the trigrams and hexagrams. They are in a state of continual transition; one changing into another, solid lines pushing outwards and breaking in two, broken lines pushing inwards and growing together.

7. Bertrand Russell. *Philosophy of the Twentieth Century.*

Chapter **13**

THE MARTIAL ARTS AND THE IDEAL MASTER

Wisdom, humanity, and courage: these three are universal
virtues for all. That whereby they are practised is one. Some
are born and know it; some study and so know it; some
through painful difficulties come to know it. But the result
of their knowing is all one. Some naturally practise it; some
do so by dint of strong effort; but the results accomplished
come to one and the same thing.
                                    —*Confucius in* Chung Yung

Recent years have witnessed dramatic changes in the practice of the martial arts on this continent. The "Karate Kraze," set afoot by superstars of television and movies, has faded somewhat; but it has also revealed the shallowness of interest and general lack of understanding of the martial arts. Many one-time sincere students have been "turned off" by cheap publicity and advertising engineered to exploit the gullible as well as giving a bad name to the martial arts themselves. Injuries sustained at the hands of unwise promoters have altered the morality and clouded the primary function of the martial arts.

When the student, despite good intentions, is caught up in this madness, the concerned husband, wife, or parent is alarmed at the disillusionment, and in some cases, broken bones, bruises, and lacerations that result from faking art.

So it is a wise student who can find a good martial arts master. Many so called masters, eager to bring fame and fortune to their particular "style" or "school," (in some cases, not least themselves!), have sold themselves and their students short, transforming them into modern gladiators, complete with protective equipment and crowds screaming for blood.

By what qualities is the genuine master known?

He is certainly no "jack of all trades, expert in none," for such a person is lacking in both knowledge and experience. The master thoroughly knows his art. It is evidenced more by what he does, quietly and unobtrusively, than by any extravagant claims he could make. If he is recognized, he will not fake a false modesty, but will admit his qualities; if he is overlooked, he will not be dejected, but go on being a master nonetheless.

A master in the martial arts is fully in control of himself. He, if anyone, is aware of his own weaknesses and strengths. What is more, he is working on the elimination of the one and the advancement of the other. He places the basic principles of the martial arts before personal desires. He displays his confidence in his succeeding, and accepts failure as only a temporary set-back on the road to success. Finally, the master contributes to the welfare of all by helping all toward good citizenship.

While there may be exceptions, it is generally true that a "master" will not reach even the lowest rung of mastership before he has diligently practised and probably taught the martial arts for twenty years or more. In addition to expert performance on the training floor, he has a prime obligation to contribute to the "state of the art" in the form of articles, essays, even books of quality that explain the cultural, philosophical, and historical traditions of his particular art and its place in the martial arts. While he is master of a given traditional technique and style, he also contributes to the arts through creative innovation, for mere imitation is not mastery. He must, as in the ancient guild system, produce his masterpiece.[1]

From the very beginning, a student in the martial arts looks to the day he will have reached mastership: the bestowal of his ninth degree Black Belt. He knows that this is no small achievement, and sets out resolutely on the way, never looking back. Naturally, mastery of self must precede any other that may follow.

The true master has glimpsed the potential within himself, and perseveringly set himself to developing it. He releases his spiritual and physical energies as an expert dancer like Vaslov Nijinsky does, as a natural form of self expression. "I am God in a body. Everyone has this feeling, but no one uses it," he wrote in his diary. The master does not deny or neglect any natural gift: all his talents are needed to make him a master in the martial arts.

A master possesses those qualities which make him a good organizer and administrator. Such a position requires a special ability—some call it charisma—to deal with others. The leader must know how to keep open the lines of communication between himself and others. He has the ability to draw out the best in the persons he works with, how to mediate conflicts, how to tap the sources at his command.

The master plays to win, of course; but winning is not his first priority. He persuades rather than forces others to right action. If he "loses," he is not unduly dejected but accepts the losses beyond his control. The greatest Master earth has ever known had, after all, a failure rate of one in Twelve. On one occasion this Master took time to define the true relationship between disciple and master. A messenger had just interrupted the Lord's speech to the people by saying that his mother and brethren were waiting for him outside. "Who is my mother and who are my brethren?" the Master replied. "He who does the will of my Father—i.e., those who follow the way I have shown—they are my mother and sister and brethren." Anyone who expects less is no master.

While exercising authority, the master is no tyrant, but models himself on the ideal.

> The over-soul is our higher self, our share in the infinite, God.
> When we are receptive to it, it possesses us, so to speak.
> Possessing us through the intellect, it is genius; possessing us
> through the affections, it is love.[2]

The master is careful to listen to others, but he is not dependent on them. This sets him apart, as no one can fully follow to his depths.

> The more conception of God, the more self; the more self, the
> more conception of God. Only when the self as this individual
> is conscious of existing before God, only then is it the infinite
> self.[3]

The master is prepared to stand isolated even in the midst of a crowd because he has the will to be the "infinite self," the embodiment of the transcendental over-soul.

Still, a genuine master in the martial arts has no need to escape permanently from society in order to preserve his innermost solitude. If that were so, it would show enslavement to his environment. The great recluse is the city recluse because he has sufficient mastery over himself not to be harried by his surroundings. Therefore, the monk, Wonhyo, returned to human society, ate meat and drank wine, mingling with lay persons without detriment to his soul.

Confucianism and Taoism find here a common link. Two extremes are synthesized in the character of the master, blending virtue in the golden mean. Confucius describes this person as one

> *possessed of all sagely qualities that can exist under heaven,*
> *who shows himself quick in apprehension, clear in discernment,*
> *of far-reaching intelligence and all-embracing knowledge, fitted*
> *to exercise rule; magnanimous, generous, benign and mild, fitted*
> *to exercise forebearance; impulsive, energetic, firm and endur-*
> *ing, fitted to maintain a firm grasp; self-adjusted, grave, never*
> *swerving from the mean, fitted to command reverence; accom-*
> *plished, distinctive, concentrative, and searching, fitted to exer-*
> *cise discrimination; all-embracing is he, and vast, deep and ac-*
> *tive as a fountain, sending forth in their due season his virtues.*[4]

Obviously, the master differs from others not by reason of his birth or class, but by his ability and character. His ideal is not illusion; he lives actively and fully.

The history of the martial arts reveals that once a student has chosen a master, he makes most progress when he establishes over the years a relationship with him that can be even stronger than ties of kinship. The highest tribute to a master is that he can sustain the loyalty of his students, for without discipleship there can be no master; without learning, there is no teaching. It is disconcerting to see students jumping from organization to organization, looking for instant results rather than mastery, for an easy time rather than thorough training. The good master knows when to be assertive, demanding full effort, and when to be patient, tolerating the slow progress of a naturally unendowed student. He inspires a sense of exhilaration in the hard-working learner, persisting in his efforts to reach perfection. "Winning" and "losing" are distinguished only in either having, or not having, tried his utmost.

The master is a person of vision. He can look ahead, gauge his student's strengths and weaknesses, and guide him in the achievement of his goal. The acme of mastery is that, while giving to others, the practitioner is finding himself. Never has one mastered an art as well as when oneis successfully teaching it. While the student is aiming at mastery, the master sees himself as the perpetual student.

The master demonstrates his art not for the sake of spectacle. He pursues it because he needs it to realize himself. The touchstone of the master is virtue. It is therefore amusing (if not pathetic) to see some indi-

viduals getting their "ranks" by mail. Experts are not made by mail order catalogue any more than astronauts are made by watching television.

No true master flaunts his trophies, certificates, and awards,
though he would not deny he earned them if occasion demanded.
Modesty is not a virtue if false. To light a candle only to hide it is waste-
ful. "So let your light shine," said the great Master, "that others may
see it" and do likewise.

Over and above cognizance of self, one needs acceptance by one's
peers—and that goes for masters, too. From this base one is positively
motivated to deeds that bring proper recognition to the martial arts.
Man does not live by bread alone; he has aesthetic needs that make him
capable of much more than eking out an existence. The master
recognizes that this is a step-by-step development which was true even of
primitive man. Thomas Gordon illustrates such a progression in *Leader
Effectiveness Training.*

> *For example, a primitive man who is hungry will be highly
> motivated to stalk a wild animal to obtain food, even risking
> his life (ignoring safety and security needs). After killing the
> animal and eating what he needs and now motivated to satisfy
> his security needs, he may cure the remaining meat and store it
> for future consumption (safety and security needs). When plen-
> ty is stored away, he might then think of asking friends to
> come over and share his food (needs for acceptance and social
> interaction). When those needs are met, he may decide to ex-
> periment with new and more flavorful ways of preparing his
> food (needs for achievement and self-esteem). Finally, if those
> needs are reasonably satisfied, he might decide to paint pictures
> of animals he has killed on the walls of his cave (need for self-
> actualization).* [5]

To move from 'caveman' to 'virtuoso' in the martial arts requires
boundless patience and much time; but that is natural, and therefore
good, for the results cannot be other than genuine and permanent.

Not everyone is a born leader; it is highly doubtful if anyone is.
There are certainly some more gifted in leadership than others, just as
there are Mozarts and tone-deaf persons. However, the door to mastery
is open to all, even as non-prodigies have become excellent musicians.
Many qualities are acquired and developed through right motivation
and persevering effort.

The martial arts master combines task specialist with social specialist. Not only does he organize and direct the external exercises of his students, but he maintains a high morale and harmony. A "leading artist" may be one, simply, who enjoys more public acclaim than another. Much greater is that "leading artist," the master, who influences other by their awareness of him. In the martial arts "leader influence" refers to a positive contribution to the attainment of personal and social improvement, and in this the master plays a crucial role in the activities of his disciples. "Leading" is the art of establishing inter-relationships between himself and his students, between one student and other students, and between students and "outsiders." The master unifies all toward a common wholeness.

In this respect the master is a facilitator or collaborator rather than a superior among subjects. The master is sometimes the best leader by "following." Human anatomical relationships illustrate the point. The brain does not despise the hand because it is less essential to the body, nor is the foot jealous of the heart because of its higher function. Each is needed by the other; the brain can send all the messages in the world, but if the hand is paralyzed, nothing happens. There is a natural hierarchy in an orderly society, but the primacy of the individual is always respected, no matter what his rank, occupation, or talent. The martial arts justify leadership only under these circumstances.

> The hero (that is, master) can be prophet, poet, king or priest
> or what you will, according to the kind of world (i.e., condi-
> tion) he finds himself born into. I confess I have no notion of
> a truly great man (master) who could not be all sorts of men.[6]

The master in the martial arts is a man of genius; he has the imagination to conceive of great plans, the ability to grasp correctly a multitude of details, and the tireless energy that keeps adapting reality to his imagined plans. Above all, he has realized within himself, and as far as possible, in others the qualities of wisdom, humanity, and courage in thought and action. He has not only allowed himself to be shaped by experience, but he has helped to shape it. In and by his "mastery" he has created with experience something uniquely personal, communal, and enduring.

NOTES TO CHAPTER 13

1. Chuang-tzu describes the secret of a certain woodcarver who upon having constructed a post on which to hang bells, was hailed by all those who looked upon it as a brilliant artist. The Prince of Lu entreated the carver to explain his secret. He replied: "I am a simple artisan and do not know of secrets. There is only one thing to be considered. When I was about to make the post, I was on my guard not to allow my energy to be diverted by any other idea. I fasted in order to bring my mind to balance. When I had fasted for three days I no longer dared think of praise or blame; after eleven days I had forgotten my body and limbs. At this time I did not even think of His Majesty's court. In this way I identified myself completely with my art, and all temptations of the outer world had vanished. After that I went into the forest and looked at the natural shape and growth of the trees. When I happened to see the right one, the post for the bells stood ready before my eyes, and I could go to work. Otherwise I would have failed. People hold my work divine because my innermost nature became merged with the nature of the material."

2. R. W. Emberson, *The Over-Soul,* From the American Tradition in Literature Vol. 1, p. 1152.

3. Soren Kierkegaard, *The Sickness Unto Death.* Translated by W. Lowrie, p. 129.

4. Confucius, *The Doctrine of the Mean,* in a source book in Chinese Philosphy, Ed. Wing-Tsit Chan (Princeton, 1963), Chapter 31, p. 112.

5. Thomas Gordon. *Leader Effectiveness Training* (Wyden Books: 1977), p. 22.

6. Thomas Carlyle. *On Heroes, Hero-worship and the Heroic in History.* (Oxford University Press, London, 1965).

Chapter 14

THE MARTIAL ARTS AND CHARACTER

...Come, my friends,
'Tis not too late to seek a newer world.
Push off, and sitting well in order smite
The sounding furrows; for my purpose holds
To sail beyond the sunset, and the baths
Of all the western stars, until I die.
                    "Ulysses" A. Lord Tennyson

In the "brave new world" presented by Aldous Huxley, everyone was engineered from conception into the "character" he was to be and the occupation he was to fill. Garbage collectors wanted nothing but to be garbage collectors; rulers could only rule by decree of the test-tube conditioning they had come from; male and female were in exact count and "role." Everyone was a robot.

A discussion of character in such a "society" would be ludicrous. Yet, to see the prevalence of conformism among groups and nations— some by choice, some by "brainwashing"—makes one wonder how many "individuals" are left in the world.

To make that number grow is the purpose of the martial arts program. Character formation is the most important duty of any individual, group, or nation. It is never finished as long as one lives.

...all experience is an arch wherethro'
Gleams that untravell'd world, whose margin fades
Forever and forever when I move.[1]

Man is the one animal that can dream. What is more, he can fulfill his dreams. Aeons before it happened, Neil Armstrong's landing on the moon had been dreamed about, written about, and studied about in science and fiction. Dreamers of the "New World" discovered it, and their progeny go on dreaming and discovering.

When "discovering" does not follow "dreaming," there is no point in the dream. Action must follow thought if the thoughts are to have effect.

My dreams are worthless,
my plans are dust,
my goals are impossible:
All are of no value
unless they are followed by action. [2]

A mediocre effort will not bring results. Whether one is chief or warrior, only an all-out application will win the prize.

This requires loyalty to one's ideals, to oneself, and to the persons with whom one is working. Loyalty is found in deeds, not in words. Rabble-rousing slogans may carry the day, but not more than a day. "The spirit gives life—the letter kills." Promises come all too easily—fulfilling them is the problem.

An obvious point of departure for loyalty is fidelity to one's instructor. A beginner in the martial arts, no less than the master, is punctual and attentive. Punctuality, it is said, is the virtue of kings—though royalty is notoriously late. Nevertheless, the punctual person is kingly insofar as he respects time: his own and that of others. Ordered conduct reflects orderly thinking; orderly thought reflects a balanced life. It is far better to spend a few hours of intense, vigorous practice than to while away many hours in mediocre activity.

Order suggests precision of organization. This is a refined form of punctuality; everything is in place, nothing is exaggerated, nothing omitted. This is the mean between idleness and hyperactivity. The acting person is in control, unifying all action toward the ultimate end.

The martial art presents the person of character as a hero, of equal stature to the protagonist of song and saga. He undertakes his work with zeal, and sticks to it until it is done. Not for him the easy expedients, the "fast buck," the "abandon ship!", given a worthy cause.

Great spirits have always found violent opposition from
mediocrities. The latter cannot understand it when a man does
not thoughtlessly submit to hereditary prejudices but honestly
and courageously uses his intelligence and fulfills his duty to ex-
press the results of his thoughts in clear form. [3]

The martial arts practitioner has the courage of his convictions. He succeeds in spite of adversity—sometimes because of it. He realizes that no civilization can fully satisfy every individual, but he is no proponent of the pill-popping generation to solve all ills. Such "relief" is short-lived at best, and only brings bigger problems in its wake. Socrates drank his hemlock, though he did not preach suicide; his action was "necessary" in the light of the convictions he had preached.

What hope for total fulfillment do the martial arts offer, one may ask, for the handicapped or the chronically ill? Here, as nowhere else so much, the martial arts philosophy shines. One must recall the definition of success in self-actualization: it is to accomplish that of which one is capable. Sometimes paraplegics and other handicapped persons achieve more than could normally be expected of even a non-handicapped person. They are proof that strong determination and persevering effort can make up for what one may lack in physique. A blind person usually compensates for his inability to see by developing his other senses to an unusual degree. Often a handicap can serve as a spur to greater determination and effort. These persons evince an unusual strength of character. Far from brooding over their misfortunes or feeling sorry for themselves, they resolutely ride the waves that might topple a weaker character, and come up with their treasure intact.

Who is to say such persons have not been "fulfilled?" Perhaps such a martial artist will not deliver many kicks or throw many punches; but he is certainly living in the spirit of the arts, first, in knowing his strengths and weaknesses; then in doing, mentally and physically, what he is capable of. Because he lacks legs, he need not lack character. Sincerity of effort cannot but lead to success.

> There are nine standards by which to govern the empire, its states, and the families, but the way by which they are followed is one. In all matters if there is no preparation, they will fail. If what is to be said is determined beforehand, there will be no stumbling; if the business to be done is determined beforehand, there will be no difficulty; if action to be taken is determined beforehand, there will be no trouble. If the way to be pursued is determined beforehand, there will be no difficulties.[4]

There is no more reason for handicapped persons to be fatalistic than there is for anyone else. If they have mind enough to know their affliction, they have mind enough to decide their own destinies. They can surely be in the driver's seat and steer themselves to a goal of their choice.

The man of character makes his life an affirmation of, not an apology for existence. He is a self-reliant hero who begins in time what he hopes to continue through eternity. The philosophy of the martial arts favors this down-to-earth approach. In nature, human beings are not "special"; a fly sits on a person's nose as readily as on a dung-heap; the tornado smashes a king as impersonally as it dumps debris. The difference in the event lies in the mind of the human, in the character of each being. The fly and the tornado practise no virtue and are guilty of no vice; the human being's actions are never without moral consequence. Victory over self-indulgence is not virtue when practised once, but when practised habitually. A gem is not polished without prolonged rubbing; so a strong character is not refined without the challenge of adversity.

The martial artist building his character fears self-deception more than he fears misunderstanding. If he is to be strong, he must continually explore himself, his goals, his values—at least as much as he explores the external world he seeks to conquer. Before he can possess the earth, he must possess himself. He must, for instance, alone and collectively, re-orient technology, his runaway brainchild, toward those goals that enhance life and restore human dignity. Possessing a skill or power is one thing: how one uses it is another. If the results are depersonalizing or dehumanizing, then the act is more accurately called abuse, and should be stopped.

> This is what we have arrived at with all our vaunted progress,
> our great technological advances, our great wealth—everyone
> goes about with a burden of anxiety so enormous that, in the
> end, our stomachs and our arteries and our skins express the
> tension under which we live.[5]

Worse is the damage to man's personhood.

In the chapter on success in the martial arts, it is pointed out that long-range goals are not only desirable, they are imperative to progress. Here it must be mentioned that the genuine practitioner does not live only "for the future." His character-building program goes on ceaselessly, and is for the present good as well as the future. The individual who is always working toward something but never arrives, is like the person who believes that the more pain he chooses to inflict on himself here, the greater something he will gain hereafter. This is masochism, not virtue.

> If this be the whole fruit of victory, we say: if the generations
> of mankind suffered and laid down their lives; if prophets con-

fessed and martyrs sang in the fire, and all sacred tears were
shed for no other end than that a race of creatures of such
unexampled insipidity should succeed, and protract...their con-
tented and inoffensive lives—why, at such a rate, better lose
than win the battle; or at all events, better ring down the cur-
tain before the last act of the play, so that a business that
began so importantly may be saved from so singularly flat a
winding-up.[6]

One returns to the golden mean: excessive self-denial (in the name of discipline or of anything else), is as unworthy (and unnecessary to strong character development) as mere whims and hedonistic pleasures. Health of mind and body is needed for efficiency in service and in character development.

The martial artist does not hesitate to scale the mountain, for only then can he view the plain. He aspires to heroism without being vain. Mysticism and practicality are elements in his character constitution, but neither in excess. No amount of abstraction on strong character will take the place of experience. The genuine artist may talk about character sometimes, but, much more, he *is* what he talks about.

NOTES TO CHAPTER 14

1. Alfred, Lord Tennyson. "Ulysses," *Anthology of Verse* (Toronto University Press: · 1964), p. 143.

2. O.G. Mandino, *The Scroll Marked IX, op. cit.,* Chapter 16, *The Greatest Salesman in the World.*

3. *Albert Einstein in a letter to Dr. M. I. Cohen, in "The Bertrand Russell Affair," New York World Telegram,* March 19, 1940.

4. Confucius. "The Doctrine of the Mean" from *A Source Book and Chinese Philosophy.* E.D. Wing-tsit Chang (Princeton, 1973) pp. 106-107.

5. W. H. Auden, "One Vote for This Age of Anxiety," *The Edge of Awareness* (Dell Publishing Co., New York: 1970), p. 96.

6. William James, *The Varieties of Religious Experience* (Collier Books, New York: 1961), p. 274.

Chapter **15**

THE MARTIAL ARTS AND SUCCESS

Chance favors only the prepared mind.
                              —Louis Pasteur

Beware what you set your heart upon,
for it surely will be yours.
                              —R.W. Emerson

The desire to succeed is universal, for no one in his right mind sets out to be a failure. What constitutes success is as varied as there are people. To one it is keeping life's priorities in perspective; to another it is being able to face himself and be proud of what he sees; to yet another it is doing what he wants to do simply for the satisfaction of doing it. Whatever the definition, success embodies a way of living that brings some kind of reward or achievement.

The Horatio Alger Awards, given annually in the United States, "honor the spirit of free enterprise,...the concept of honesty not only in private life but...in professional life; they celebrate the continued vigor of a nation that honors those citizens who have turned adversity into triumph."[1]

Obviously, success does not fall out of the blue: it is something that must be earned, the result of some endeavor. It is not a point in time or a geographic location in space, but is an on-going process of "becoming" rather than of "having". It is possible for anyone in the world, no matter where, why, or what the circumstances for that person. Everyone is capable of doing something: even "failures" serve (it is remarked): they are bad examples to the rest!

In the martial arts, the practitioner does not waste time worrying and fretting over what he can *not* do: he works on what he *can.* He realizes that everyone is endowed with the seeds of greatness in some form and to some degree. He may be the only one to see what that is, but that does not lessen the greatness.

"Heaven is not reached by a single bound," says the poet; so success: it too, is reached step by step, moment by moment. Therefore, the martial artist arms himself with an unending supply of patience.

Also, "success" may come to mean different things at different times. To a child, success is having all the sweets he wants; later his ambition is to be a fire-chief; still later, he graduates to success in his studies or on the job—and so on. Therefore, a certain flexibility in attitude is necessary. One comes to events beyond one's control: death in the family, an unforeseen opportunity, an accident, or an inheritance. What one does control is the way one reacts to such events, how one thinks about them. Here one's attitude is all: if positive, it can mean changing disaster to triumph; if negative, it can mean the opposite.

What the martial artist does from the start is set his goals, long-range and short-range. The latter are set into perspective with the former, so that he may climb naturally, rung by rung. His goals are worthy, are of permanent value (in the long run), and look to the welfare of the *whole* person. They are realistic in terms of his abilities and limitations. They are within the laws of God and man, in accord with his conscience and potential.

To order these objectives, the practitioner defines his values as clearly as possible, reviewing these from time to time, adjusting and modifying as occasion and his growing maturity prescribe.

The martial artist founds his values and goals on living in the present, at this time, in this place. There is not much good in sentimental nostalgia for the "good old days," nor in the always-jam-tomorrow futures that never happen. The rags-to-riches image followed by so many can be a mirage if it refers only to material wealth. Whatever the plan, it is lop-sided if it panders only to one part of human needs.

The mature practitioner has learned to make his own decisions and accepts the consequences of them, for weal or for woe. Naturally, risks are involved because one is subject to error; but the advantages far outweigh the risks. Mistakes, properly handled, can be turned to advantage; or at least one can learn not to repeat the same ones.

> *This is a confusing world we live in. At every turn we are forced to make choices about how to live our lives. Ideally, our choices will be made on the values we hold; but frequently we are not clear about our own values.*[2]

ʃ The martial artist lives and acts on the belief that others are basical-ly well-intentioned and decent. His dealings with them will reflect this belief, at least until he is given incontrovertable evidence to the contrary.ʒ Trusting others will bring trust in return. Experience teaches that one does come into contact with some misguided persons, but one need not accept their values or judgments. Important to the practitioner, however, is consistency of "values"; that is, he does not get into a flap over the slaughter of seal-pups for their fur, and then vote for abortion-on-demand legislation. That is straining the gnat and swallowing the camel.

There are some choices that originally seem right but subsequently prove undesirable. If these are of the type that can be changed or aban-doned mid-course without great harm or inconvenience, they may not have been so bad, as they help the individual gain experience. The long-range goals, however, that take one well into life and become ir-revocable must be more carefully weighed before made or abandoned. These goals must be both true and noble, or one's life will be empty, no matter how "successful" one may appear to be.

An example comes to mind from Arthur Miller's play, *The Price*. Two brothers are reminiscing over career choices they made. Walter, the "successful," now wealthy doctor, is speaking to his policeman brother:

> *"I never had friends—you probably know that. ... You start*
> *out wanting the best, and there's no question you need a cer-*
> *tain fanaticism; there's so much to know and so little time. Un-*
> *til you've eliminated everything extraneous—including people.*
> *And of course the time comes when you realize that you*
> *haven't merely been specializing in something—something has*
> *been specializing in you. You find you've become an instru-*
> *ment that cuts money out of people. And finally it makes you*
> *stupid; power can do that."*[3]

The martial artist's march to success never walks over other people; determination he has, but not fanaticism; personal achievement is a goal, but not "by hook or by crook"; wealth, maybe, but not by "cut-ting it out of people."

The martial artist has a clear picture of the kind of person he wants to be, the identity he wishes to associate with his personality. His plan of action must then flow as the authentic expression of this identity. The pursuit of his plan is self-directed; his short-term goals are ordered within his life-long ideals. He views life as a kind of constant combat, as did Paul when he said, summing up his life's work, "I have fought the good fight, I have finished the course."[4]

Combat in the martial arts teaches many a hard fact about life. It can certainly teach the individual a great deal about himself and others. To be a success he needs not only the means to carry out his intentions, but the knowledge that he has the means, and the confidence that he can carry them out. This is useful not only to the practitioner, but is an encouragement to those around him; confidence is infectious, just as discouragement and pessimism are.

The martial artist is not above seeking for and accepting help in time of difficulty. "Failure" is not at all intolerable when one's relationships are secure. Because the practitioner's life is directed by choice, not chance, he has sought and established close friendships. As a rule, one associates with those who hold interests and attitudes similar to one's own. Having high ideals means that one's associates have likewise high ideals. They are likely "winners," and by association, influence one to be the same. Thus, one's chances of success are enhanced by the friends one chooses.

A genuine martial artist never lays the blame for his setbacks at someone else's door. This would be escapist. He knows he can, and should, monitor his own behavior by turning inward. If what he finds is displeasing or impractical, he re-programs his plans, and proceeds from there.

To do this intelligently, one must be perfectly honest with oneself and others. It may be necessary to recall often that the individual best realizes his success in aiding the success of others. The circle of these "others" may be limited to one's family, friends, or immediate neighbors; or it may be as broad as the world community; whatever one's capacity and one's effort to fill it, that is the extent of one's success.

Pertinent to this establishment of relationships is the multi-level nature of a well-founded group. These choices are free from bias, stereotyping, and myth. One of the most vocal subjects today is the male-female relation: what ideals of equality are just, practical, desirable? The martial artist fearlessly examines tradition, explores proffered alternatives, accepts personal challenges in the assigned sex-roles. If economic and medical realities (not to mention superstitious beliefs) reveal false premises as to physical strength, emotional stability, mental and spiritual capacities, the honest person is resolute in following through on the practical level. Short of biological differences, men and women hold equal chances of success in the martial arts program. One likes to believe that the caveman's survival mentality has come a long way in dissolving sex biases on the way to success. Ideally choices are made on the basis of qualifications and ability rather than on accidental genital appendages.

All these ideas fundamentally affect the image one has of oneself. If one is type-cast from infancy as weak, submissive, and unstable (the "traditional" female), one tends to make this a self-fulfilling prophecy. If one is encouraged from the beginning to be strong, assertive, and intellectually active, this is likely the kind of person one will become. In any case, the individual's achievement (or success) is in direct ratio to her/his motivation (or drive), based on his/her self-image (or potential). High achievement in any field need not spell a lack of femininity for a woman active in a traditionally male role, nor an emasculation for a man exercising his right in a traditionally female role. Male nurses and female railway-engineers have every right to success if this is their choice. The martial arts philosophy is fertile soil for the cultivation and refinement of these values in the achievement of goals, for success does not depend on "fate" or "accident".

The successful martial artist is certainly a specialist, an expert in his field. But he is not tunnel-visioned, incapable of any other activity outside his immediate specialty. This would be an assembly-line mentality in which one mechanically affixes rear-view mirrors, for example, and knows nothing more about the automobile. Too often top positions are unattainable not because the person lacks talent, but because he chooses to be "over-specialized." The well-rounded engineer not only builds good bridges, he has an appreciation of fine music. This is not to disparage expertise, but to applaud the "total man", the person capable of some degree of success wherever he finds himself.

If over-specialization is detrimental, a word of caution may be given on over-success. An excess of wealth or power, for instance, may cause its owner to become obsessed with it, and so be side-tracked from more permanent (life-long) ideals, such as self-improvement.

If I had but little knowledge
I should, in walking on a broad way
Fear getting off the road.
Broad ways are extremely even,
But people are fond of by-paths.
The courts are exceedingly splendid,
While the fields are exceedingly weedy,
And the granaries are exceedingly empty.
Elegant clothes are worn,
Sharp weapons are carried,
Foods and drinks are enjoyed beyond limit,
And wealth and treasures are accumulated in excess.
This is robbery and extravangance.
This is indeed not Tao.[5]

The enjoyment of food and the possession of wealth are obviously not in themselves evil: their excess is.

In sum, success as defined in the martial arts is founded on a normally healthy,[6] able, self-confident person's sincere search for happiness. He/She is free from the obsession of "success" in whatever form it may come. Happiness and fulfillment result from unselfish service. To serve at one's best, one must have a balanced energizing force of mind, body, and spirit. The philosophy of the martial arts recognizes that man is not only *a member* of world society, but also that he is a member *of society*, where the common good and private fulfillment are inextricably interwoven. To harm one is to harm all; the well-being of all is the well-being of the one.

NOTES TO CHAPTER 15

1. *Success Unlimited,* June, 1978 (Vol. 25, No. 6), Chicago, p. 31.
2. Sidney Simon et al, *Values Clarification* (Hart Publishing Co.: 1972).
3. Arthur Miller, *The Price* (Dramatist Play Service Inc.: 1969).
4. *New Testament,* II Tim. 4:7.
5. Lao-tze, *Tao Te Ching, op. cit.,* 53.
6. The Constitution of the World Health Organization defines health as follows:
   (It is) a state of complete physical, mental, and social well-being, and not merely the absence of disease or infirmity.
   The enjoyment of the highest attainable standard of health is one of the fundamental rights of every human being without distinction of race, religion, political belief, economic or social condition.
   The health of all peoples is fundamental to the attainment of peace and security and is dependent upon the fullest co-operation of individuals and States.

Chapter **16**

TRAVELING WITH HOPE

*There exists no more difficult art than living. For other
arts and sciences, numerous teachers are to be found
everywhere. Even young people believe that they have acquired these in such a way, that they can teach them to
others: throughout the whole of life, one must continue to
learn to live, and, what will amaze you even more,
throughout life one must learn to die.*
                                              —Seneca

Accumulation, interpretation, and application of beliefs, principles, laws and knowledge about man, the universe, and reality give
purpose, meaning, and direction to life. From these it is possible for
each individual to formulate his life's objectives and to use them as
directional posts to guide his steps and shape his destiny. Each person,
whether or not he realizes it, has such a personal philosophy. The way
one thinks and talks, what one does, how one reacts to others, their
return reactions—all indicate one's philosophy of life.

It may be very difficult to express on paper what one's philosophy
is. This task is highly recommended, however, for it clarifies thought,
belief, and attitude. It may come as a shock to some to discover what
actually motivates them, what results their actions have, or that their
goals are only illusions. One's source of power may be weak while the
objectives sought are worthy; the source of power may be strong, but
the objectives unworthy; or, best of all, the source of power is strong
and the objectives worthy.

Realizing self by following the way of the martial arts depends very
much on the strength of one's drives and the worthiness of one's aims.
Without these, the individual is a rudderless ship, drifting aimlessly, going nowhere, and always in imminent danger of shipwreck.

Whatever one does is done to realize oneself. Persons act to secure
some desirable end or object. Does this mean that one aims at a series of
states of the self, discontinuous and fragmented? Certainly not; for one

aims at the sum of these states, a sum to which each particular state contributes. The question is to find the true whole.

Self-realization is not narcissistic self-seeking. Even achieving a full
knowledge of self is insufficient to live completely. One cannot always
be taking and never giving; in order to learn well, one must teach. To
find happiness, one must make others happy. To realize self, one must
"realize" his fellow travelers on the way. This is the whole toward
which one's acts are directed. Every choice is related to that unity in
diversity which stands above the particular choice. The aim is not unity
only, for that is static; nor diversity alone, for that is chaos; but both,
integrally realized in the other.

The true self rightly wills what is for the individual's good. Personhood includes certain forces or inclinations that are antagonistic to
the true self. These elements constitute the "other" within, that the true
self must control. Unless this is accomplished, there is no mastery.

While the way one lives and the way one defines self are intimately
related, they are not synonymous. External constraints and circumstances can limit the way one lives; but the inner personality knows no
such constraints. At every moment, consciously or subconsciously, the
individual chooses what he *is* as a person, though he may not show ex-
ternally what he is. Not to choose—that is, to change—is also to have
made a choice.

The martial arts point out that a better world begins with a better
self. Charity does, indeed, begin at home. Self-realization consists partly
in the synthesis and coordination of daily experience, and partly in the
development of innate spiritual capacities. Both processes, however, involve the full use of all talents and endowments, great and small.

A key feature in such realization is that, as a moral agent, one is
responsible not only to oneself, but, by association, to society. Those
who seek pleasure selfishly are those who gain little pleasure in life. The
hedonistic paradox is inevitably perpetuated by ego-centrism. On the
other hand, the recognition and supplying of legitimate needs is a part of
self-fulfillment.

Striving in the martial arts program presupposes at least a minimal
freedom, both from external force and from internal impulses. Some
designate these impulses evil, others call them "primitive," still others

try to dismiss them altogether as unconscious or subconscious. Whatever the view, only a minimally "free" person can exercise will in harmony with the highest standards of human conduct. While basic freedom is not possessed by all, it is a freedom of which the possessors cannot be deprived by external situations.

To exercise free choice is said in the martial arts to be heroic or virtuous. Again, it is not enough that an individual strive for it; he must also effectively want it for everyone else—that is, look for social perfection. This requires self-discipline, often leading to the sacrifice of individual pleasure or satisfaction. Whether one decides to be this or that kind of person is up to the individual, but no one can escape the choice. To commit oneself to the martial arts is to be committed to those principles by which one makes morally consequential choices.

Responsible dedication is more a matter of will than of reason. Many persons know the way, but will not to follow it. Reason clarifies the nature of commitment, leading to a fuller awareness of optional alternatives; arguments for and against a course of action must be weighed. But the final responsibility for choice rests on each person alone.

Therefore, to avoid choosing arbitrarily it is necessary to learn what is objectively to be done. What may be good individually—i.e., being "wealthy"—may not be good socially—i.e., when one's neighbor is starving. To "realize" oneself is good, but not at the expense of another. Thus, personal virtue is also social virtue. This the martial arts insist upon.

Granted, to achieve all this is no easy matter. To realize social perfection often depends on the willingness of others as much as on the efforts of the individual. The "good life," in the view of others, may be the pursuit of honor, wealth, or power. While these in themselves are not evil, they are still only useful as a means to an end, and not as ends in themselves. To resist the temptation of getting caught up in the means takes great courage, as long ago Aristotelean ethics point out.

> *Although courage is concerned with feelings of confidence and of fear, it is not concerned with both to an equal extent, but deals more with situations that inspire fear. For he who is unruffled in such situations and shows the right attitude toward them is more truly courageous than he who does so in situations*

that inspire confidence. In fact, men are called courageous for
enduring pain. Hence, courage is a painful thing and is justly
praised, because it is more difficult to endure what is painful
than to abstain from what is pleasant.[1]

But how can one "enjoy" virtue if virtue is painful? In the first place, not all virtue is painful; when it is, it is for the sake of a greater good, as the momentary pain of surgery brings long-lasting relief—indeed may save a life. The practice of virtue depends on clear judgment, self-control, symmetry of desire, and artistry of means. The martial arts do not see virtue as the possession of a simpleton, nor the gift of the innocent, but the achievement through experience of a mature person. It is, to say it once again, to follow the golden mean.

Excellence in living, as in the martial arts, is won by training and acquiring sound habits, for virtue and right action are mutually reinforcing. It is by acting conscientiously that one arrives at the mean. Daily thoughts and actions not only exemplify one's personal philosophy, but certainly also influence the philosophy of the martial arts. The ultimate objective for both general philosophy and that of the martial arts is intrinsically the same: to produce the most useful citizen, the total human. As has been shown, the approaches to achieving the objective have different emphases. The martial arts stress the spiritual and physical, general philosophy stresses the intellectual. On the premise that the wholeness of personhood must act in totality, both philosophy and the martial arts are present in every action of the practitioner. The *whole* person goes to school, not just his intellect; the *whole* person blocks and kicks, not just his hands and feet.

The philosophy of the martial art is a philosophy of life. It charts one's professional course of thought and action, progressively and intelligently. It employs both motor activities (chiefly concerned with muscle strength) and mental activities (concentration and meditation). It affords experiences in related areas, such as health and recreation; it provides the opportunity for moral development, emphasizing honesty, fair play, cooperation, and patience; it enhances social action, encouraging communication and understanding. The martial arts promote progressive phases of self-perfection for the purpose of developing responsible world citizens.

A just world will become possible only when it becomes meaningful also to those millions of people whose very existence is no more
than a daily battle to keep alive. The bedrock of the martial art is a
healthy society, made up of healthy individuals; the deadly technique of
self-defense is merely a by-product of an imperfect world. Hence, the
modern martial artist cannot ignore the miseries around him, but must
learn to cope with such realities as disease and starvation, and (as far as
possible) remove them or lessen their effects.

From the viewpoint of martial arts principles, it is particularly
puzzling that the weapons against human ills in the Western world are
drugs, prescriptive medicines, and surgery when the main killers and
cripplers in developing countries are beyond the reach of such remedies.
Ninety percent of the ailments afflicting impoverished people are clearly
definable and would respond to relatively simple, safe treatment. The
vast resources spent on remedies might be much more effectively used
on prevention.[2]

This does not mean that medical research should be discontinued:
the martial arts strongly favor progressive thinking. As times change, so
do the needs. "Do the best you can, wherever you are, with what you
have, all the time." (T. Roosevelt). Dr. Albert Schweitzer directs his
daily activities by the principle "reverence for life." "Live and help
live" to the martial artist means, "I will share with you what I have."
Such living will effect a health society, for everyone looks up to willing
workers, doers, leaders. The urge to service is central to the practice of
the martial arts.

Clearly opposed to this practice are plunder, greed, and selfishness.
Epitomized in such action are the slogans "might is right," and "what's
mine is mine if I can take it." Persons acting thus are demanding what
they have not won. They give nothing, produce nothing, yet expect
everything. They are moved to take their pleasure where they find it, to
"live it up" today because tomorrow is uncertain.

The philosophy of the martial art condemns the action of those
who try to get what they want and do what they please with little or no
regard for justice, order, love, or truth. It cannot be the guide for the
"gimme" and "I wanna" mentality. Surely this is not the kind of person
who can be depended on to give new life, new ideas, values of integrity,

industry, leadership, and wisdom to the world. He does not have them himself: how can he give them?

Even morality, in the martial arts philosophy, is but one facet of life; its laws are developments of natural law, and so must change as life changes. These laws condition the modes of self-defense as they have developed in the struggle for existence among individuals and groups. All life, by definition, strives to endure and grow; moral life is the inevitable self-conscious stage of the resulting development. Such life is not measured chronologically, but in scope, complexity, and depth of experience. As biological, psychological, and sociological sciences become more exact, a healthier moral system is possible. To "have life and have it more abundantly" is the end of the martial arts.

No distinction of quality can be recognized without destroying the value of the exact quantitative method. The breadth of life, which is recognized as one of its dimensions, means not so much width of rationally interesting activities or the development of a broadly human point of view, but variety and intricacy of activities insofar as these promote well-being. If conflict were to arise between these two dimensions (length and quality of life), so that the individual were forced to choose between them, it would seem that the fundamental principle of self-defense demands the sacrifice of length to quality. In the absence of any fixed measuring unit, the very concept of quantity of life remains even more indefinite than the pre-scientific idea of the greatest happiness, which it was devised to supplant.

However, the ultimate goal of the martial art is not achieved by sacrificing either breadth or length of life. The morality of the martial artist is not the slave's way of surviving, but the mastery of life. The ideal is not to satisfy any momentarily expedient law, moral or political, but to bring new value, new morality, new norms to society. The artist is concerned with Aristotle's "high-mindedness."[3]

Additionally, Nietzsche's doctrine fits the martial arts philosophy insofar as he makes use of the notion of struggle and survival to support this thesis. Nietzsche makes "will-to-power" the essence of personality. The intellect and its creations have no independent value, but are instruments in the service of this instinct to life. It is the glory and excitement of the struggle itself, the sense of strength, that make the effort

worthwhile. To eliminate this struggle, to make life overly comfortable
and safe, is to take from it that which gives it much of its charm. Hence,
fadistic social morality and so-called "religions" reduced to sympathy
and renunciation are to be condemned as encouragements to weakness
and debilitation. The slave-morality of the unthinking herd is to be
replaced by the master-morality of the higher man. Its supreme command is: "Be and do!"

The philosophy of the martial art affirms the martial artist as a person of prestige if, and only if, he is this high-minded man who deserves
much. The defining properties of superior morality have already been
discussed as strength, solitude, courage, and perseverance. These render
a person capable of feats beyond the call of ordinary individuals. The
martial artist is consistently what he is, not just on some single, for-
tuitous occasion. There must be more than accident or impulse in the
contest between any hero and his adversary, his task, or his fate.
William James writes:

> When a dreadful object is presented, or when life as a whole
> turns up its dark abysses to our view, then the worthless ones
> among us lose their hold on the situation altogether...But the
> heroic mind does differently...it can face them if necessary,
> without for that losing its hold upon the rest of life. The world
> thus finds in the heroic man its worthy match and mate...He
> can stand this Universe.[4]

Courage is often associated with a willingness to die. What does
death mean to the martial artist? To him it is a practical problem. Suzuki
points out that "what (the hero warrior) wanted was not to be timid
before death, which they had constantly to face. This was a most practical problem on their part, and Zen was ready to grapple with it, probably because the masters dealt with the facts of life, and not with
(mere) concepts."

Indeed, a person's readiness to die is by itself sufficient to raise him
above those who are not, provided he does so for a cause worthy of
such a sacrifice. "No matter what a man's frailties may be," continues
William James,

> if he is willing to risk death, and still more if he suffer it hero-
> ically in the service he has chosen, the fact consecrates him for-
> ever. Inferior to ourselves in this or that way, if yet we cling to
> life and he is able to 'fling it away like a flower,' as caring

nothing for it, we account him in the deepest way our
born superior. [5]

The heroes of Greek myth, depicted as facing death with a grim awareness, would appear to be the signal instance of the above description. Yet they are, none of them, careless of life in the way the statement implies. Achilles, when death after all had overtaken him, and his spirit had gone to Hades, said, "Rather would I live on ground as the hireling of another, with a landless man who has no livelihood, than bear away among all the dead that be departed." The meanest life on earth seemed preferable to the highest place among the earth-departed.

What distinguishes the hero's view of death from the ordinary man's is his determination to force the issue, to place his life on the line—something that he could, if he chose, avoid. He does this partly because he knows it is expected of him, that his position demands it. The honors accorded him, and withheld from lesser men, are in recognition of his willingness to give them up. So the martial artist is taught that dying with convictions is better than living without any.

Finally, it must be said that the person who lives by instinct rather than conviction is shut up within the circle of his private interests; family and friends may be included, but beyond that nothing is regarded except as it may help or hinder what comes within the circle of his instincts. In such a life there is something feverish and confined, as compared to the calm, free life programmed for the martial artist. Such a private world, set as it is in the midst of great and powerful forces, must sooner or later be left in ruins.

Unless one can transcend the narrow interests of self, one remains like a garrison in a beleaguered fortress, knowing that the enemy prevents escape, and that ultimate surrender is inevitable. In such a life there is no peace, but only constant strife between the insistence of desire and the powerlessness of the will. In one way or other, if life is to be great and free, escape from this prison is imperative.

The martial arts show the means to freedom through contemplation. This is not to divide the universe into two hostile camps— friends and foes, good and bad, helpful and hindering. Rather, contemplation leads one to view the whole impartially, with no part beneath consideration.

All acquisition of knowledge is an enlargement of self, best attained if not directly sought. It is obtained only when desire for knowledge and practice are both operative, when that operation does not wish in advance that its objects should have this or that character. In the process of development it adapts the self to achieve its potential from within. The mind that has become accustomed to the freedom and impartiality of philosophic contemplation will preserve something of the same freedom in the world of action and emotion.

The martial artist in his completeness as a rational, volitional, and moral being, as well as one who is sentient and appetitive, can effect the realization of his higher self in any way otherwise unattainable. To become a true warrior in any martial art, as in the combat of life, is his unswerving endeavor. The principles of the martial art thus merge with the principles of life itself.

NOTES TO CHAPTER 16

1. *Nichomachean Ethics,* op. cit., p. 76.
2. The philosophy of the martial art brings to the health problems of this generation the traditional approach of Oriental health promotion. These are within everyone's reach, rich or poor, peasant or king, weak or powerful, as they are based on breathing techniques; meditation, and exercise—basically a method of prevention and self-cure. Without a view to health, how can one hope for better life? (See also "Notes to Chapter 16," #6.)
3. High-mindedness is concerned with great and lofty matters...A man is regarded as high-minded when he thinks he deserves great things and actually deserves them; one who thinks he deserves them but does not, is a fool, and no man, insofar as he is virtuous, is either foolish or senseless...A person who deserves little and thinks he deserves little is not high-minded, but is a man who knows his limitations. For high-mindedness implies greatness, just as beauty implies stature of body. *(Nichomachean Ethics).*
4. William James, *op. cit.,* p. 333.
5. *Ibid.,* p. 336.

SELECT BIBLIOGRAPHY

BOOKS

Artistotle. *Nichomacheon Ethics* (Bobbs-Merrill, New York: 1962).

Albert et al. *Great Traditions in Philosophy* (van Nostrand, New York: 1975)

Arneil, Steve, and Bryan Dowler. *Karate: A Guide to Unarmed Combat* (Coles, Toronto: 1975)

Bonsall, B.S. *Confucianism and Taoism* (Epworth Press, London: 1934).

Camus, Albert. Speech of Acceptance Upon the Award of the Nobel Peace Prize for Literature, December 10, 1957, trans. by Justin O'Brian (Knopf; New York: 1958).

Capra, Fritjoh. *The Tao of Physics* (Chaucer Press, Bungay, Suffolk: 1975).

Chau, Wing-tsit, translator and compiler. *Chinese Philosophy* (Princeton University Press: 1973).

Chen, K.H., compiler. "Hu Shih and Chinese Philosophy," *Chan's Essays* (Oriental Society: 1969).

Cho, Sihak Henry. *Korean Karate: Free Fighting Techniques* (Charles E. Tuttle, Tokyo: 1968).

Confucius. *Mencius, translated by L.A. Lyall (Longmans-Green, New York: 1932).*

_____ *The Sacred Book of the East*, Vol. 28, translated by James Legge (Motilal Banarshidass, Delhi: 1068).

_____ *The Analects* in *The Human Way in Ancient China: Essential Works of Confucianism,* edited and translated by Ch'u Chai and Winberg Chai (Bantam Books, New York: 1965).

Corcoran, J. and Emil Farkas. *The Complete Martial Arts Catalogue* (Simon and Schuster, New York: 1977).

Delza, Sophia. *T'ai Chi Ch'uan: Body and Mind in Harmony* (Good News Publishers, North Canton, Ohio: 1961).

Dennis, F., and P. Simmons. *The Beginner's Guide to Kung-Fu* (Pinnacle Books, New York: 1974).

Eliade, Mercea. *Myths, Dreams, and Mysteries* (Harper and Row, New York: 1957).

Fromm, Erich. *Escape From Freedom* (Avon Books, New York: 1965).
_____ *The Sane Society* (Rinehart, New York: 1955).

Fung Yu-Lan. *A History of Chinese Philosophy,* Vol. II, translated by Derek Bodde (Princeton University Press: 1953).

Giles, Herbert A., translater. *Chuang-tzu: Mystic, Moralist, and Social Reformer* (Shanghai: 1926).

Gluck, Jay. *Zen Combat* (Ballantine Books, New York: 1976).

Harvey, M.G. *Self-Defense by Judo* (Coles, Toronto: 1975).

Huang, Al Chung-liang. *Embrace Tiger, Return to Mountain* (Real People Press, Moab, Utah: 1973).

Ilyon. *Samguk Yusa* (Legends and History of the Three Kingdoms of Korea), trans. by T.H. Ha and G.K. Mintz. (Yonsei University Press, Korea: 1972).

SELECT BIBLIOGRAPHY

BOOKS

James, William. *The Varieties of Religious Experience* (Macmillan Publishers: 1961).

Killanin, Lord, and John Rodda, editors. *The Olympic Games* (Collier Macmillan Canada: 1976).

Kiss, Michaeline. *Yoga for Young People* (Archway, New York: 1973).

Langer, Suzanne K. *Feeling and Form* (Charles Schribner Sons, New York: 1953).

Lao-tze. *Tao Te Ching,* translated by R.B. Blakney (New American Library, New York: 1955).

Lawson-Wood, Denis. *Chinese Systems of Healing: An Introduction to Acupuncture* (Health Science Press, London: 1951).

Lee, Jae M., and David H. Wyat. *Hopkido, the Korean Art of Self-Defense* (Arco Publishers, New York: 1976).

Logan, W. and Herman Petras. *Handbook of the Martial Arts and Self-Defense* (Funk and Wagnals: 1975).

Maier, Henry W. *Three Theories of Child Development* (Harper and Row, New York: 1965).

Manners, David. *Teach Your Child Self-Defense* (Arco Publishers, New York: 1976).

May, Rollo. *Man's Search for Himself* (W.W. Norton, New York: 1953).

Nicol, C.W. *Moving Zen: Karate as a Way to Gentleness* (William Morrow Co., New York: 1975).

Nietzsche, Friedrich. *Beyond Good and Evil* (The Modern Library, New York: 1971).

Russell, Bertrand. "Freedom and Government," *Freedom: Its Meaning,* edited by R.N. Anshen (Harcourt-Brace, New York: 1950).

Rutt, R., editor *History of the Korean People* (Taewon Publishers, Seoul: 1972).

Scheler, Max. *Man's Place in Nature,* translated by Hans Meyerhof (Farrar-Strauss, New York: 1961).

Shim, Sang Kyu. *Promise and Fulfillment in the Art of Tae Kwan Do* (17625 West 7-Mile Road, Detroit: 1974).

Smith, Huston. *The Religions of Man* (New American Library, New York, 1958).

Soko, Yamaga. *Sources of Japanese Tradition,* Vol. I, compiled by R. Tsunoda et al. (Columbia University Press: 1958).

Steiner, Claude. *Scripts People Live By* (Random House, New York: 1957).

Suzuki, David T. *Mysticism* (Harper and Row, New York: 1957).

——————— *Zen Buddhism,* edited by William Barrett (Anchor Books, London: 1956).

——————— *Zen and Japanese Culture* (Pantheon, New York: 1959).

SELECT BIBLIOGRAPHY

BOOKS

Takao, Chu, translater. *Tao Te Ching* (Buddhist Society, London: 1937).

Tsunoda, R. *Sources of Japanese Tradition* (Columbia University Press: 1964).

Tyler, Martin, editor. *The History of the Olympics* (Marshall Cavendish Publications, London: 1970).

Watts, Alan. *Tao, the Watercourse Way* (Pantheon Books, New York: 1975).

Welty, Paul T. *The Asians: Their Heritage and Their Destiny* (J.B. Lippincott, New York: 1966).

Wright, Arthur R. *Buddhism in Chinese History* (Stanford University Press: 1959).

PUBLICATIONS

The Atlantic Monthly, Vol. 246, No. 3 (September, 1980), "A State of Grace: Understanding the Martial Arts," Don Ethan Miller.

The Globe and Mail (Toronto), Broadcast Week Magazine (August 2-8, 1980), "History Turns Full Circle," Dick Beddoes.

GLOSSARY

ahimsa: the doctrine of non-violence practised by Hindus and Buddhists.

aikido: a Japanese method of self-defense which took root from the jujitsu style. Founded by Morihei Uyesheba, 1942, Tokyo; based on non-resistance with an assailant. Uses opponent's forces against him.

Analects, The: thoughts and sayings of Confucius, collected and recorded by his disciples.

anatta: a no-soul doctrine found in Buddhism. Budda rejected the notion of a human soul.

arhat: a holy man, freed of all desires, and so having reached enlightenment.

art: a form of self-expression; the most perfect way of doing something. By definition, its evolution is continuous; therefore, never stale, never boring, never merely repetitious or imitative.

bando: a system of fighting used in Burma. Consists of various karate-related techniques of striking with the hands and feet blocking and countering.

bushido: the way of the warrior, a code of ethical behavior followed by the samurai. Main principle was loyalty to one's lord. Today bushido provides the ethical background for the martial arts and is claimed to account for such virtues as humility, honor, and discipline.

ginseng: a Chinese perennial herb whose aromatic root is valued for its medicinal qualities.

hwarang (warriors): a band of 18th century Korean patriots who, much like Japanese samurai, adhered to a strict philosophical and moral code of art known as hwarang-do, "the way of the flower of manhood."

I Ching: the Chinese Book of Changes. Its main principle is that the strong changes to gentle, and the gentle to strong.

Jen: brotherly love or compassion, the highest of all Confucian virtues.

Judo: "gentle way," a method of unarmed combat developed from jujitsu by Jigoro Kano. It embraces five stages of instruction, each containing eight throws. For every throw there is a proper counterthrow involving definite principles of motion.

jujitsu: early Japanese hand-to-hand fighting, both armed and unarmed, characterized by rudimentary kicking, striking, joint-locking, throwing, holding, choking; from it, aikido and judo took their roots.

kami: any type of supernatural being or force, held as a Shinto belief.

karate: "empty hand" fighting; the Japanese have four major systems of the art: 1) shotokan; 2) shito-ryu; 3) wado-ryu; 4) goju-ryu. Its most effective techniques include the reverse punch, the side-kick, the spinning heel kick, and the ridge hand.

kendo: modern art of Japanese fencing performed with bamboo swords. Is based on the development of only seven efficient blows and one thrusting technique. Literally, "way of the sword."

kobudo: "weapons way," the art of Okinawan weaponry practised in conjunction with various styles of karate in their advanced stages. The different weapons are improvised from farm instruments or tools.

GLOSSARY

kung-fu: a Chinese martial art based on the movements of animals (bird, bear, monkey, etc.). The inner teachings are much more important than the physical techniques (e.g., hand and foot movements). There are hundreds of subdivisions of the art. Popuarlized on this continent by Bruce Lee and the Kung Fu television series. Its birthplace was the Shaolin Temple. Basic movements come from imitating the crane, the dragon, the leopard, and the snake.

kwonpup: an early Korean method of unarmed combat, popularized in Korea from 1147-1170. Later developed into tae kwon do, the most popular Korean martial art today.

mana; an impersonal supernatural force or being, believed to exist in certain types of animate and inanimate objects.

numina: powerful, invisible forces believed by ancient Romans to exist everywhere in nature.

samadhi: a trance-like state of super-consciousness, the ultimate goal of yogic meditation when the mind loses all awareness of self.

sambo: Russian form of wrestling similar to judo.

shaman: in modern terms, a medicine man or a witch doctor; someone believed to have special powers and the ability to deal with supernatural matters.

style: an individualized method of performance. Basically, the Japanese straight lines; the Chinese circular motion; the Korean emphasis on kicks (other than punches or locks).

tae kwon do: Korean martial art has many sub-divisions such a hapkido, hwarang-do, kwonpup, and others. Is one of the most popular forms of unarmed martial art in the world.

tai chi chuan: a martial art easily identified by deliberate, slow-motion exercises that are continuous, circular, and rhythmic. Speeded up, it is unquestionably a self-defensive art.

vajramushti: a fighting art existing in India before 1000 B.C., used by the warrior class of that time.

wakan: a supernatural force revered by the Sioux Indians; a being similar to mana.

wu-shu: "war arts," an encompassing term for Chinese martial arts. More recently known as unwarlike, self-expresive, and physical fitness arts of the "new" Chinese society. Is basically kung-fu.

yudo: the Korean form of judo; practically no difference between it and the Kodokan judo taught in Japan.

APPENDIX

THE MARTIAL ARTS AND THE OLYMPICS

To many, the Olympics represent the ultimate in athletic competition. The "nobility" and "greatness" of human skill are extolled; the internationality of its participants is touted as a uniting force among nations engaged in friendly competition.

Why, then, are the martial arts not a part of it?[1]

To understand the answer in the context of the martial arts presented in this text, one must look at how the XXII Olympiad of 1980 evolved from pre-Olympic and Olympic times.

The first recorded Olympiad dated from 776 B.C. The ones before this time were a part of religious and cultural ritual rather than a strictly athletic event. Olympia (the gathering place for competitors), grew in size and importance, attracting artists of every kind: poets, sculptors, painters, musicians, historians. Beauty of body, soul, and mind held the primacy of pursuit.

All too soon, however, deterioration of this spirit set in, political power and wealth reared their Medusa heads. When the Roman Emperior Nero, for instance, entered, he was "allowed" to "win" the chariot race. So much for honest competition! Indeed, fines were imposed on individual cheaters if discovered, but this did not stem the tide of politicking: In 393 A.D. the Olympics were entirely abolished by decree of the emperior Theodosius.

Fifteen hundred years later, they were resurrected by someone primarily interested in their educational value. Pierre de Coubertin convinced an international group in the Sorbonne in 1894 that the games should be re-instated. His intentions were of the highest order:

> *Why have I restored the Olympic Games? In order to*
> *ennoble and strengthen sports in order to assure their indepen-*
> *dence and duration and thus to set them better to fill the*
> *educational role which devolves upon them...*
> *Having wished to renew not so much the form as the prin-*
> *ciple of this thousand-year institution because I saw in it for*
> *my country and for humanity an educational orientation which*
> *had become necessary, I had to seek to restore the powerful*
> *fibre which had strengthened it in the past; intellectural and*
> *moral fibre.*[2]

Physical, intellectual, and moral education were to go hand in hand. And so it seemed to do—for a while. But alas for the high idealism of humanitarians! Wars and jingoistic nationalism lurk everywhere, forever eroding what is best in humanity.

What tallies does the Olympic scoreboard flash to date? There have been triumphs, of course; but of their spirit, it seems little remains. Behind the scenes are horror tales of corruption, drug-abuse, racial prejudice, political intrigue. Ideals have been replaced with ideologies; the good of the athletes is totally subordinate to the whims and vagaries of economics and of politicians. Security precautions have reached the ludicrous—steel fences and hundreds of thousands of police—that yet fail to prevent terrorism and murder. The whole spectacle has become hypocritical, a huge pretense of feigned peace and harmony, of sportsmanship, of "healthy" competition.

The most deep-seated cancer eating at the vitals of the Olympics seems to be its involvement in petty (or gross) politics. Hitler used the Olympics as a staging stunt for Nazism and the spawning of his Aryan super-race aberration. Moscow boycotted these competitions in 1936, organizing a counter-competition in Spain, in protest of Nazi tyranny. The Russians, in fact, did not participate in any Olympiad until 1952. In 1980, it was Moscow's turn to suffer boycotts by approximately one-third of the current number of contesting nations, led by the United States, in protest of Russia's invasion of Afghanistan. And so the sordid details continue.

What have the martial arts to do with such double dealing? (What, one might well ask, has any decent citizen to do with such disregard of human rights?) The genuine martial artist must answer: nothing! That is not to say, that nothing should ever be allowed to happen until all conditions are perfect; obviously, very little would be allowed to take place. However, honesty in admitting imperfections, and willingness to correct these effectively is not beyond even limited human beings.

The martial artist's values are above the empty vauntings of political power, wealth, and personal prestige. For him, the prime competition is always and foremost with self; this "winning" and "losing" are determined by "honest" or "dishonest" effort. What is bad for the soul (i.e., immoral), is bad for the body. Contrariwise, virtue is good for both. No true martial artist could have any part in the travesty made (in the name of Olympics) of fair play, good will, and the welfare of the total person. He could not suffer the kind of "breeding" and "rearing" of individuals that goes on, as though they were so many prize beefs, or worse, trained to become destructive robots. Unfortunately, the Olympics have taken on such ungainly proportions as to make them self-destructive. Athletes represent considerable financial "investment" for the sponsor—not to speak of the sacrifices the athlete himself makes in personhood and individuality. Investment demands financial returns, not sportsmanship.

There are exceptions, of course. Not every Olympic competitor is a pawn of the state, any more than every "martial artist" is the next thing to God. However, the basic philosophy and end results show irreconcilable contradictions. The martial arts promote a way of life (as opposed to gaining one skill); they advocate what is natural (as opposed to what is unnatural); they look to the development of the whole person (as opposed to developing only his body, or certain parts of it); they are directed to social well-being (as opposed to selfish individualism); they have no axe to grind (as opposed to ulterior political one-upmanship). The Olympic "rings of destiny" have too often become the manacles of basic freedoms, as Amnesty International can only too potently testify.

Any activity, including sport, can be turned to weal or woe. If competition can develop impartiality, honor, and be a spur to chivalrous effort, then: long live competition! But if it leads to corruption, villainy, and a win-at-all-costs attitude, then the world of competition is in a bad way.

The clarion call of the martial arts sounds unequivocally for the healthy mind in the healthy body, the dedication of soul and spirit to honest conviction, and the fulfillment of high principle in effective action.

NOTES TO APPENDIX

1. Judo was introduced in 1964, but the martial arts as a whole were absent.
2. Pierre Coubertin, *Une Compagne de vingt-et-un ans,* quoted in "The Founder of the Modern Games," by Marie-Therese Eyquem, *The Olympic Games,* edited by Lord Killanin and John Rodda (Collier Macmillan Canada: 1976).

INDEX

INDEX

INDEX OF AUTHORS